Olive Custance in about 1902

The Inn of Dreams

The Inn of Dreams

by

OLIVE CUSTANCE
(LADY ALFRED DOUGLAS)

Edited and introduced

by Edwin J. King

Saint Austin Press, London.

MMXV

First published, London and New York, 1911.

ISBN 978-1901157697

DEDICATION

J'ÉCRIS POUR QUE LE JOUR OÙ JE NE SERAI PLUS

J'écris pour que le jour où je ne serai plus
On sache comme l'air et le plaisir m'ont plu,
Et que mon livre porte à la foule future
Comme j'aimais la vie et l'heureuse nature.

Attentive aux travaux des champs et des maisons
J'ai marqué chaque jour la forme des saisons,
Parce que l'eau, la terre et la montante flamme
En nul endroit ne sont si belles qu'en mon âme.

J'ai dit ce que j'ai vu et ce que j'ai senti,
D'un coeur pour qui le vrai ne fut point trop hardi,
Et j'ai eu cette ardeur, par l'amour intimée,
Pour être après la mort parfois encore aimée,

Et qu'un jeune homme alors lisant ce que j'écris,
Sentant par moi son coeur, ému, troublé, surpris,
Ayant tout oublié des épouses réelles,
M'accueille dans son âme et me préfère à elles.

COMTESSE MATHIEU DE NOAILLES

CONTENTS

For my mother
Who told me recently :
" I don't feel like an old lady.
I am still just a girl of sixteen
inside my head. "
E.J.K.

Introduction

This modest critical edition of *The Inn of Dreams* is a personal tribute to Olive Custance from an admirer of her poetry on the occasion of the seventieth anniversary of her death.

I am an English teacher and have simply thought it a useful exercise to present, in my endnotes, each poem in a pedagogical way. My approach in teaching, and here, is to provide a certain number of keys to allow the pupil to open up the different levels of meaning in a poem. It is necessarily a rather directive process and there is obviously a danger that the teacher traps the student into his own way of looking at a text ; this is indeed true of all art and of all teachers.

But in our day, western culture's common language of signs and symbols has broken down. Even in English literature courses at our universities, professors are obliged to present a general overview of the classics, of historical periods (especially in thought) and an introduction to the Bible, before moving on to the study of individual authors. Our common language of culture is, regretfully, disintegrating.

So better a directive approach than no help at all ; without help, a great many readers could be left with the impresssion that these beautiful poems are even more obscure than they are meant to be ; and in fact, although Custance was influenced by Symbolism (where a series of images and ideas present a vague atmosphere without a particular message or story) most of her work actually displays a clear narrative structure. Sometimes one just has to read a poem two or three times to realise it. And, because when a poet makes an allusion he is borrowing strength and meaning from another source, one needs to understand the many allusions which Custance makes in order to enjoy the full force of her poetry.

So I have provided some biographical clues and information on allusions to other writers and to ancient mythology. As the poetess was heavily influenced by Catholicism at the time of the original publication of this collection (1911), and was - in her own way - religiously inclined all her life, I have included explanations of some important Christian imagery and language.

Because I am convinced that there is a kind of progression in the poetry of this particular collection, and that the selection and ordering of the poems expresses a kind of personal story, I have added nothing, nor have I taken anything away. For the same reason, I have felt it admissible to provide my own tentative commentary and interpretation in order to help readers understand the story as it unfolds.

It seems to me, in fact, that this collection presents a tale of movement from darkness to light ; from youth to middle age; from religious doubt to a tentative but mature Christian faith. There is also, as Nancy Hawkey has observed, a movement from "pronounced sensuality" to a "mood of disillusionment", but this is partly down to the fact that as she grew older, she began (like her husband) to tire of the mood she had struck in the 1890s and struggled to keep up ; she lacked "the stamina to maintain the Decadent posture."[1]

Some critics have opined that *The Inn of Dreams* was a rehash of previously published work with little new material; for them, her days as a poet were ended by 1911, killed off by her marriage. Then again, other critics had damned her previous work as immature, imprecise, vague and too *honeyed*. Certainly her earlier poetry was incapable of achieving a consensus among critics, except for the complaint that she used to many pointless elipses[2]. In the selection made in 1911, we see a sifting taking place. And we also see perhaps the exclusion of poems that Custance may have become uncomfortable about not just because of their quality but also because of their themes.

The Inn of Dreams was in fact published at what may seem, with hindsight, a time when Custance combined happiness with maturity ; when she was, in a sense, in her prime. Even if it is true that it was also a time when the storms were gathering and her

---

[1] Nancy J. Hawkey, 'Olive Custance Douglas : An Annotated Bibliography of Writings About Her' preceded by an 'Introduction', in *English Literature in Transition, 1880-1920*, vol. 15, No. 1, 1972, pp . 49-56.
[2] An annoying habit, even more present in her correspondence.

'fairytale' was about to hit trouble, as she seems to sense especially keenly in several poems, and notably in *The Prisoner of God*. This collection represents Custance's own summing up of herself and her work at a time when she was taking stock of her life. It is for these reasons that I have thought it a useful exercise to bring out a critical edition of her last collection. Father Sewell certainly did a great service to literature in producing a volume of her *Selected Poems* about twenty years ago ; but this is now difficult to obtain and the selection inevitably reflects his own tastes. I have preferred to give the snapshot that Olive herself decided to offer of her mature poetry.

Perhaps it would be a useful exercise to bring out a critical edition of her 'Collected Works', bringing together the contents of *Opals* (1897), *Rainbows* (1902), *The Blue Bird* (1905) and the present selection, *The Inn of Dreams* (1911), together with various uncollected pieces from magazines, newpapers, correspondence and her diary. This is indeed a hope that Father Sewell expressed. If nobody else beats me to it, I hope I shall do this in the next year or so. Because of that I will especially welcome constructive criticism on any and all aspects of the current publication.[3]

But before we delve too deeply into her poetry, we need to know more about its author. Who is this free spirit who wrote freely and generously of her love to so many of her friends and even slight acquaintances, who was remembered for her 'flower-like beauty' and 'radiant charm', and signed herself *wild Olive* ?

Olive Custance (1874-1944) is a popular figure in the footnotes of the collected works of various late Victorian writers and in articles published by modern gay rights activists. In death, as in life, she remains very much in the shadow of her husband, Lord Alfred Douglas, who can be described as *famous* or *infamous*, according to the different criteria which different people employ when making such judgements.

The best modern account of her husband's life is that of Caspar Wintermans, if one can pardon Wintermans for a tone

---

[3] The Editor can be reached at the following address : Chavagnes International College, 85250 Chavagnes en Paillers, France.

which sometimes moves beyond forgiveness and into sentimentality with regard to his subject. Not much, however, has been written about Olive Custance. Most people who have heard of her today can only tell you that Oscar Wilde's ex-boyfriend married her when he was 'on the rebound', or that *she* married *him* on the rebound from a lesbian affair, and perhaps that they had a disastrous marriage which snuffed out her poetic muse.

The problem is, however, that *none* of this is strictly true.

Here, in a necessarily concise version, is her story ...

Born at 12, John Street, Berkeley Square, Mayfair in London (7th February, 1874) to a respectable landed family with an estate at Weston Old Hall, Weston Longville near Norwich, she was introduced into London society at a relatively young age. Her father, Lieutenant-Colonel Frederic Hambledon Custance of the Grenadier Guards, inherited the Norfolk estate from his father in 1892 and the parents and two daughters moved there, when Olive was 18. But the family kept up a London house too, enabling her to continue to move in both aristocratic and artistic circles in the capital.

In 1890, when she was 16, she met the strikingly handsome 25-year-old John Gray, a self-educated poet of London working class origin who translated much *fin de siècle* French poetry into English as well as writing fine poems of his own. He had, when they met, only just become a Catholic. From 1891 to 1893 he conducted an intense and possibly sexual friendship with Oscar Wilde at which time he lapsed from Catholicism, only to return to the Church in 1895, eventually becoming a priest in Edinburgh. He is reputed to be the inspiration for Wilde's *The Picture of Dorian Gray*, but this in fact seems to be unlikely. When Custance met the man she became infatuated with him and wrote poems about him, calling him her 'Prince of dreams'. He was, in fact, her first *boy muse*. He subsequently maintained a correspondence with Custance, advising her about her work, and he sent her a Christmas gift in 1894 of five poems he had written in honour of the Christchild.

With assistance from Gray and others, Custance soon gained acclaim as a poet and became a regular contributor to the *Yellow Book*, a publication which regrouped the work of the main literary figures of the English *fin de siècle* ('end-of-the-century'), and also included important translations from French.

Custance's poems were published in three main collections : *Opals* (1897), *Rainbows* (1902), *The Blue Bird* (1905), and lastly *The Inn of Dreams* (1911).

Brocard Sewell, in a short biographical monograph[4], calls Olive Custance one of the 'three principal women poets' of the period, with Dollie Radford and Alice Meynell.

She is, especially in her earlier poems, representative of that *fin de siècle* period characterised by 'a hothouse fragrance; a perfume faint yet unmistakable and strange.'[5] It is certainly a period which, in English letters, was much influenced by the Decadent movement in French literature. It included a kind of eroticism containing a 'mingling of what is effeminate in both sexes'[6]. Custance joined this milieu at sixteen and was swept along by it, even if with her, Decadence "was more of a fleeting phase or mood than a deliberately cultivated attitude".[7]

When one considers the whole of Custance's work, in fact, it is clear that she wears the badge of *Decadent* rather lightly, and perhaps mainly due to her assocation with certain key Decadent figures. Much of Olive's poetry is not about the typical Decadent dimness, crimsons, purples and golds (colours not only suggestive of royalty, but also of an eastern brothel or opium den), but about "pink roses, tender green plants, soft rain and new love ... butterflies ... delicate autumn days ... beauty personified."[8] The misattribution of the term Decadence to Custance, rather than perhaps simply the identification of *a certain aetheticism*, is as much the fault of her contemporary critics as it is of modern ones. There is also the problem that anyone who finds himself (or

---

[4] Brocard Sewell, *Olive Custance : Her Life and Work*, 1975.
[5] Holbrook Jackson, *The Eighteen Nineties*, 1913, p. 197.
[6] Jackson, op. cit. p. 197.
[7] Sewell, op. cit. p. 16.
[8] Hawkey, op. cit., p .50.

herself) situated anywhere close to the massive shadow cast by Oscar Wilde, is likely to be subsumed and obscured by it, as we shall see.

Wilde was indeed the key figure in the fin de siècle literary scene in England. And it was to another passionately intimate friend of Wilde's that Custance turned her attentions in 1901. Lord Alfred Douglas, or 'Bosie' to his family and friends, was the delicately handsome young man with whom Wilde had conducted a scandalous affair, landing Wilde in Reading Gaol, after a series of embarassing court appearances triggered by the public disapproval expressed by Bosie's father, the Marquess of Queensberry and by Wilde's own arrogance.[9] On Wilde's release from prison in May 1897, Douglas went to spend some time with him before his death in November 1900. Wilde had asked to make a sixth month spiritual retreat with the Jesuits on leaving jail, but his request was refused. In the event, he died of a brain haemorrhage, sickened by alcohol, but was received into the Catholic Church on his death bed. The two men who buried him, Robert (Robbie) Ross and Lord Alfred Douglas, were both to become Catholics later. But first, Douglas was to meet and marry our poetess, Olive Custance.

In late 1900 and early 1901 Custance became involved in a friendship with the overtly lesbian writer Natalie Clifford Barney in Paris, which Barney later included in her memoirs. Barney had first made overtures to Custance, in writing, after reading her first collection of poetry, *Opals*. Custance accepted an invitation to Paris where Barney and an English girl going by the name Renée Vivien were trying to set up a 'Sapphic community'. Despite claims, however, that Custance had a sexual affair with one or both of these two women, there is a total lack of real evidence to support it. Barney was something of a predatory lesbian who sought (and indeed had) sexual encounters with many attractive and artistic young women. She was also very charming.

---

[9] Wilde had sued Queensberry for libel, but the evidence given by male prostitutes at the trial led to Wilde's susbequent conviction for gross indecency.

Modern lesbian scholars are still very keen to enlist Custance in a kind of Sapphic community of the spirit, even after her death. And yet the facts do not really bear it out. The young Olive visited Paris in spring 1901, accompanied by her mother and the future ninth Earl of Sandwich, the Hon. George Montagu.[10] Natalie Barney claimed that at this time Olive tried to persuade her to marry Bosie in a *marriage blanc*, to form a kind of *ménage à trois*, but that this was stymied by the jealousy of Barney's current lover Renée Vivien who apparently threatened Barney with a pistol.[11] This proposal of a three-way marriage sounds more like Natalie Barney's fantasy than Olive's. Or else Barney was exaggerating a half-joking flirtatious remark of the kittenish[12] *wild Olive*.[13] Barney liked to brag and (no doubt) exaggerate about her lovers before an extensive audience, as many men also do. Olive had no such propensity.

After staying a month in Paris, Olive's mother allowed her to holiday in Venice with Barney and Renée Vivien for a month, accompanied also by a chaperone who enjoyed the maternal trust,[14] as Mrs Custance had formed a strong dislike for Barney. She need not have worried: Barney later complained that Olive spent much of her time looking at a photograph of a statue of Antinous (the Emperor Hadrian's deified boy-lover) because it reminded her of Lord Alfred, with whom she was already deeply in love, although the two had not yet even met.[15] Also, both

---

[10] Although Caspar Wintermans (2004) seems to think it was another aristocrat and family friend, Henry Frederick Walpole Manners-Sutton, the future Lord Canterbury, who was with them. Perhaps they were both there.

[11] Wintermans, op. cit., p. 100.

[12] Sewell's phrase, op. cit.

[13] As she signed herself in some correspondence to friends.

[14] Yet who apparently spent most of her time in bed with an Italian sailor.

[15] He was also the inspiration for her poem 'Antinous', published in *Rainbows* in 1902. To give a little more context : the poetic love of statues was a popular literary conceit among certain homosexually inclined poets of the late 19th century as it allowed for a kind of 'chaste' homoeroticism, addressed to marble.

Natalie and Olive were ill with a malarial fever for most of the holiday.

There is certainly an effusive admiration, and even flirtatiousness, in a poem written by Custance to Barney[16], but nothing to equal the sincerity and ardour of what she wrote at about the same time to Lord Alfred Douglas with whom our poetess simultaneously began a really very serious courtship[17]; one which she herself instigated by writing to him admiringly in June 1901, about six months after the death of Oscar Wilde. When they met, after her 'fan letter' to the rather unhappy Douglas, it was more or less love at first sight. She wrote often and with a sometimes disarming simplicity: "If I were to write for ever I should never be able to tell you how much I love you."

Douglas' reaction to Olive's devotion was not quite what she hoped at first, for although he was falling in love with her, he had financial worries and decided to sail to New York in the autumn of 1901, in search of a rich wife. He wrote to her that he was a great success with the American ladies. One of them was, it is claimed by various authors, Natalie Barney, who had returned back home to her father in the USA and presumably floated the *ménage à trois* idea again. Barney's father wanted her to marry, but opposed the union, it seems. Despite what is affirmed by some writers, they were never engaged.[18]

---

[16] In an uncollected fragment, quoted in Sewell (op. cit. p. 12) in reply to Barney's initial letter of appreciation for the first collection *Opals*, Olive writes playfully of those who have played with 'some sweet mad sin ... Twixt maid and maid'. But that is all.

[17] It has been suggested that the Bosie connection had actually fired Natalie's desire for Olive. *Natalie and Romaine: The Lives and Loves of Natalie Barney and Romaine Brooks*, Diana Souhami (2012), p. 10.

[18] (For flatly contradictory versions of this episode, see *Chère Natalie Barney: Portrait d'une séductrice* by Jean Chalon (1992), and *Women Artists and Writers: Modernist (im)positionings* by Bridget Elliott and Jo-Ann Wallace (1994), p. 33. Caspar Wintermans (2004 and (2007), always exhaustive in every way, merely claims that Bosie and Barney *saw a lot of each other* and *got on quite well* during his stay in America.

Olive also wrote, teasingly, that some European ladies had been chasing her. This was a reference to Renée Vivien (real name, Pauline Tarn), the jealous lover of Natalie Barney. Vivien, who had previously told Barney that Olive was 'trite, like all English girls' was staying in London with her mother, Mrs Tarn, and so she arranged to meet Olive. On this occasion they, at the very least, kissed and embraced, which was probably a normal proceeding with Olive for male and female friends.

Vivien then wrote a gushing letter to Olive, on 31st October, telling her that she loved her : "You have brought me nothing but roses ... the roses of Sappho. You are a melody, a perfume, a light, a song. - My lips once more mingle with your lips in the depths of sweet memory. My lovely Love, I am yours for all my life."[19] Olive's reaction was to forward the letter to Bosie in America. Bosie, who thought this gesture 'rather unkind'[20] responded by insisting she write and reassure him that she loved him more than she loved Renée. Olive quickly answered that indeed she loved him better than anyone else in the world.

But this temporary separation from Lord Alfred Douglas drove her not into the arms of the Parisian Sapphic ladies' circle, but instead into one of those of the young family friends who had taken her out there to meet them : heartbroken, she acceded to parental advice and became engaged to the Honourable George Montagu. He was a young, handsome, recently elected Member of Parliament, heir to both a peerage and a large fortune.

It should be explained that the main problem with the relationship between Bosie and Olive was that neither thought the prospect of marriage realistic, although they loved each other. Bosie, in particular, was beginning to understand the need for financial security. He had squandered in just over a year most of the £15,000 he had inherited from his father in January 1900 ; had he been more careful, he might have lived comfortably off the interest. But now he had no other financial prospects. The

---

[19] Quoted by Caspar Winterman's Introduction to I Desire the Moon, the Diary of Lady Alfred Douglas 1905-1910, 2004, p. 10.
[20] According to Wintermans (2004), op. cit, p. 14.

disgrace of the Wilde trials also meant he would have been unlikely to obtain the consent of Olive's father, even if he had money. And yet, as Lord Alfred Douglas was still aboard the ship sailing to America, he began to realise that he could not spend the rest of his life away from the woman he now knew he loved.

When Bosie returned in January 1902 he was horrified to hear of Olive's engagement to Montagu, who was an old school friend of his ; unlike Bosie he had an income of £30,000 a year and good prospects, and Olive found him amusing ; he even did very good impersonations of Bosie, and Olive enjoyed acting and joking with him.

Perhaps part of the horror sprang from jealousy, but there was also the fact that George Montaigu was one of the few friends who had stood by him during the Wilde scandal (they were in fact extremely intimate for a while), but had then abruptly dropped him (on advice from friends) in order to run for Parliament. He was a kind of Judas for Bosie.

Bosie grasped the bull by the horns and proposed a rash and romantic way out. Their love, which had essentially been brought to flower in romantic correspondence and a very few actual meetings, now burst into radiant and passionate life : the two eloped and married in a discreet service at St George's, Hanover Place in March 1902, without Colonel Custance's consent, and with a honeymoon in Paris. George Montagu's family was furious ; even the King was dismayed by the proceeding. But Montagu was stoical and after a few years himself married an American heiress, as was the fashion for English aristocrats at that time ; although in his case it was not because he needed the money. He later became an expert on the history of trains ; which, if nothing else, is certainly conclusive proof that Olive would have tired of him rather quickly.

It had been, all things considered, the most eventful and romantically complicated year of Olive's young life so far. And although the record of odd entanglements and childish caprices of both young people over the previous twelve months did not give cause for great optimism as to the prospects of such a marriage, it somehow lasted, with dramatic highs and lows, for 42 years. About eight months after the wedding, Olive gave birth to their first and only son, Raymond in November 1902.[21]

In 1905[22] Olive published this poem, 'To My Husband' in which she touchingly sees herself as binding up all his wounds of suffering with her playful kisses and songs :

> I sing the joy and sorrow of the world,
> The strange and secret histories of the heart ;
> I am a dreamer, and each day my dreams
> Go out to kiss the eyes of lovely grief,
> The laughing mouth of Love. I have bowed down
> Before the light of beauty all my life,
> And now, O poet passionate and brave,
> O lover with the beautiful sad face,
> Like a shy child I bring you all my songs.

Later, in 1907, Bosie wrote a series of six sonnets to Olive, in which he announced " Now I have known the utmost rose of love. "

His attraction to her was to her sylph-like beauty which awoke in him a masculine force that he had not really felt before. He wrote that when he saw her in London, stricken with the news of her engagement to Montagu, " the blood of a hundred Douglas ancestors surged up. " Ironically, for Custance, she loved him as a *boy-prince* ; it was precisely his youthful, effeminate beauty that attracted her. As soon as they were married, Bosie " deliberately tried to be more and more manly "[23] but the more manly he became, so Bosie claimed, the less attractive he was to Olive. She wanted her beautiful fairy boy, her Antinous, while Bosie wanted to close the chapter of his previous adventures with Wilde and Ross.

However, despite the fact that she may have delighted in having in her arms a youth who was equally attractive to a good

---

[21] And, surprisingly, Natalie Barney seems to have been the godmother at the child's (Anglican) christening.

[22] As the dedication to her collection, *The Blue Bird*.

[23] Quoted in Sewell, op. cit., p. 20.

many men, she did not enjoy thinking about the more sordid aspects of Douglas' homosexual past. She disliked Robbie Ross, for example, the other famous lover of Wilde, and was always worried about learning " something dreadful " through the " dastardly attentions of blackmailers, letter-sellers and information-mongers "[24]. She was by now a moral conservative, just as her husband was quite soon after the death of Wilde.

It has been suggested by some especially prurient scholars that the couple did not have sexual relations after the first few months of their marriage. The evidence adduced is that they only ever had one child, probably conceived before the wedding. The only plausible explanation for this ludicrous claim springs from the way in which modern attitudes are so different from those of the early twentieth century. Many people now seem to view homosexuality as a kind of divine vocation : *once a homosexual, always a homosexual.* For such minds, once Bosie and Olive had experienced the love of someone of their own sex, no durable happiness could be possible elsewhere ; and in any case, just as the modern press will congratulate male celebrities who 'come out of the closet' and ditch their wife and family, so the marriage of Bosie and Olive was (the argument runs) a betrayal of their true selves and therefore a sham, all evidence to the contrary notwithstanding. And the evidence to the contrary is plentiful.

Bosie had at least two serious affairs after their marriage, both with women, and during his affair with Miss Doris Edwards, an American, he (by now a Catholic convert) wrote to Olive blaming her for *forcing him to commit to mortal sin.* By this, he meant that he experienced such a strong sexual need for his wife that he had to find comfort elsewhere, and with another woman. This in fact triggered a change of heart with Olive who welcomed him back into her arms shortly after reading the letter.

Admittedly, a lot of the confusion comes from a few stray lines in Alfred Douglas' own *Autobiography*[25] which are interpreted as stating that Olive was a lesbian who could not really love a

---

[24] Lord Alfred Dougas, *Oscar Wilde and Myself*, 1914, Pp. 181, 209.
[25] Quoted in Sewell, op. cit., p. 20.

man. Apart from the fact that Bosie was not exactly a reliable witness on questions of sexuality, as he had changed his mind about it many times and was capable of some incredible distortions, one needs to look squarely at what he actually says. My reading is that in the early stages of their marriage Olive loved him with the kind of sexual hunger that one would, at the time, have associated more with young men than with young women. And her passion was linked to her vision of him as a beautiful young boy. But Bosie says that although a certain heat came out of their love as he grew older and more manly, a 'different kind of love remained'. He does not suggest for a minute that she was unhappy with him because he was not a woman, simply that she was less passionate. Perhaps Bosie did not know that this is actually the common experience of married people.

In Olive's 1905-1910 diaries we discover that they had separate bedrooms, but this was in fact the norm for upper class couples at the time. She mentions visits from Bosie in the middle of the night and sometimes wishes he were with her at night when he is away. But they were independent, eccentric people. Even in 1908 she is already musing that it would be charming *if Bosie and she had a house each and visited each other every day.*[26]

I will give my honest impression of the couple and their sexuality, for what it is worth. Bosie was emotionally immature as a young man, was very close to his mother, whom he addressed in letters from school as 'My own darling' ; by the time he reached Oxford he had come to be revolted by the brutishness of his father. His own parent's marriage was a farce : his father, a keen boxer, used to brag to his wife of his trysts with prostitutes and eventually suggested she join him with his mistress in a *ménage à trois* ; the marriage ended when his saintly wife successfully sued for divorce. This meant that Bosie had no real first hand experience of normal married love. For him, the "carnival of unbridled lust'[27] which he apparently experienced in boarding

---

[26] Wintermans (2004), op. cit., p. 84.

[27] Quoted in Caspar Wintermans, *Alfred Douglas : A Poet's Life and His Finest Work*, 2007.

school at Winchester College[28], continued while he was at Oxford ; and Oscar Wilde, caught up in the excitement, gave him every encouragement. Bosie was really capable of quite incredible immaturity (his friend George Bernard Shaw said he *vacillated between age five and fifty*) and so he remained for many years in what for men of his background was usually the passing phase of *public school nonsense*.

Writing of the beginnings of his friendship with Wilde, Douglas wrote :

> Even before I met Wilde I had persuaded myself that "sins of the flesh" were not wrong, and my opinion was of course vastly strengthened and confirmed by his brilliantly reasoned defence of them, which may be said to have been the gospel of his life.... [A]t that time [I was] a frank and natural pagan, and he was a man who believed in sin and yet deliberately committed it, thereby obtaining a doubly perverse pleasure.... Inevitably, I assimilated his views to a great extent. [29]

Oscar Wilde and Lord Alfred Douglas were, for a time, at the vanguard of a nascent homosexual liberation movement ; but it was at a time when not only was homosexuality being clinically documented for the first time but also in fact being tentatively invented as a new mode of being (as opposed to an embarassing weakness). Since at the time its self-understanding owed much to ancient Greece, it was in fact a philosophy that combined a high doctrine of 'spiritual' love between an older and a younger man with the cheerful indulgence of lapses into the exercise of baser desires, often with male prostitutes, and often rather young ones. It adopted the Greek model uncritically ; the modern ethic that sex, or even just romantic love, ought to be between 'equals' was quite absent from the world of Wilde and Bosie. Bosie, as is

---

[28] His best friend at Oxford had been the poet Lionel Johnson, who had also been at Winchester College. It was Johnson who introduced him to Wilde after lending him Wilde's *The Portrait of Dorian Gray*.
[29] Lord Alfred Douglas, *The Autobiography*, 1929.

obvious from his early verse, had no qualms about "the consumption of boys as commodities."[30]

This meant that from any modern point of view, whether orthodox Christian or secular humanist, the *Hellenic* world of the 1890s was a place of sordid hypocrisy as well as of idealism and beauty. It is true that the Marquess of Queensberry (Bosie's father) was himself an advocate of free love and boasted of his visits to (female) prostitutes ; true also that hypocrisy about sexuality was to be found in many places in Victorian society. But two wrongs do not make a right ; and the homosexual side of the aesthetic movement was distinguished by the paradoxical combination of supposed superiority over the common man and a total lack of feeling or principle when it came to male prostitution.

Despite the desperately immoral sexual life Bosie led as a young man, however, where *being naughty* with boy prostitutes around the world was becoming more and more of a habit, his experience, with Wilde, of a deep love between two human beings perhaps made him slowly begin to think of the idea of marriage and its lifelong commitment ; and also about true love, as opposed to sex or friendship.

In meeting Olive he found the key to unlock the grown-up man that had been waiting to emerge. He listened for perhaps the first time to a strong, masculine voice within himself, and then that voice grew stronger. He loved and desired Olive, by his own admission, almost at first sight[31]. His love for her meant that he could also begin to listen to another inner voice, the voice of his Christian conscience. And that religious voice – which is evident in his poetry even years before[32], but which he had sought

---

[30] Jane Stevens, 'Self-pity, doggerel and beastliness' in *The Daily Telegraph*, 10th May 2007.

[31] Sewell, op. cit., p. 20.

[32] Such as in *Rejected* (1896), when he writes while languishing in Paris and pining for Wilde, 'I will have none of Christ, and Apollo will have none of me' ; but periodically also cries out for God's help, such as in *Lust and Hypocrisy* (1894) : 'When will God come, and, with his fearful fan, Purge this rank harvest and turn night to day ?'

to stifle - also grew louder over the next few years. This is why he was able to turn the corner on his homosexuality (and, painful to remember, his pederasty). He later said of himself that he had always been orthodox : *first an orthodox pagan, then an orthodox Catholic.* His (re)conversion to Christianity was completely in earnest. There was no turning back to his old life.

Olive, on the other hand, was much less complicated in terms of her sexuality, even if her personality was, like an opal, full of different colours and moods. Moderns suppose that because she fell for an effeminate young man she must have been hopelessly sapphic in her inner core, and would have preferred a life with a woman at her side. But the truth is that she liked boys just as much as Bosie did, and sought to romanticise her particular devotion to male youth in poetry. But there was nothing sordid about her devotion ; she loved both the body and the soul of John Gray and Alfred Douglas, her *fairy princes.* She was drawn to companionship and fidelity, and to a spiritual union as well as to beauty ; she was not, like Natalie Barney or indeed the young Bosie, much interested in serial sex, even if one can sometimes form that impression from stray lines in her diary, correspondence or poetry. Perhaps the playful young Olive may have, as Barney claims, spent one night in her arms. But if she did, one night was enough for her. She wanted a man or, rather, a boy. And, indeed, she thought of herself as a girl – as a fairy princess. So what could be more natural ?[33]

References to the beauty of various women in her diary strike me as normal for a sensitive and artistic woman. All the romance is about Bosie, not about her female friends. Even when she claims in her diary, half-heartedly, that she and Bosie have grown bored of each other, she muses that she might want to look for another *fairy prince,* not a *princess.* And when, later, she covers him with kisses *because he looks particularly golden,* it is he who tires of it before she does.

---

[33] "See! What a child I am!" she wrote. "But you will understand because you are a child too, my Darling... my own Bosie whom God made for me, I think." Quoted in Stevens, op. cit.

One needs also to remember that Olive was a woman from a privileged background at a time when that was a very difficult role play. Without the previous generation's codes of religion and duty which might have given meaning to her life, and having flirted with the excitement of the Decadent *pose*, Olive was completely cut adrift and prone to a profound *ennui*, especially during the period described conversely by Bosie as "the happiest of our married life" : March 1906 to January 1908.

During this time Olive was left isolated in a quaint farmhouse near Salisbury while Bosie spent much of the time away on business in London and elsewhere. Olive left the care of her son to the nanny and the cooking and housework to other servants. She had nothing to do and, according to her diary, spent an enormous amount of time in her room feeling sorry for herself. A medical problem with her ears is not enough to account for the many days on which she writes : 'spent the day in bed'. Also, at this time, she had more or less stopped writing poetry, although she had plenty of leisure to do so. For a woman of thirty-three, Olive Custance, at least in the intimacy of her diaries, comes across as incredibly immature. The changes of mood are rather tedious even if strangely endearing ; Bosie probably felt the same about them.[34]

Still, such speculations do not really help to discover the true root of difficulties in their marriage, nor do they answer the equally important and intriguing question of how the marriage did in fact survive, despite " the welter of mud and stones "[35] hurled at it over a period of forty years.

Bosie blamed different people at different times (including his wife and son). The weight of evidence suggests that the main causes of marital instability were : the constant revisiting of the business with Wilde in the libel courts (litigation continued long after Wilde's death, and Bosie seemed to have acquired a

---

[34] Another of Olive's admirers before her marriage, Richard Le Gallienne, was enchanted by her 'girlishness' but soon realised that he would not be able to cope with a lifetime of it.

[35] Lord Alfred Douglas, *The Autobiography*, 1929 ; quoted in Hawkey, op. cit.

taste for it), the fate of their son Raymond, the interference of Olive's father, intermittent lack of money and, lastly, Bosie's own difficult temperament.[36] Indeed one scholar observes that after 1902 Olive disappeared from the social scene and expended most of her energies "in coping with her husband."[37]

But the early years of the marriage were, nonetheless, described by Olive as 'radiant'.[38] Initially, it seems, things went quite well, even with Olive's father. Colonel Custance forgave Bosie's failure to seek his consent to the marriage and welcomed them both at Weston, where he taught Bosie how to fish. A son was born quickly, in November 1902.[39] There followed a period of relative marital bliss and success for both Olive and Bosie in their literary lives. Olive published collections of poems in 1902 (*Rainbows*) and 1905 (*The Blue Bird*)[40].

Bosie became editor of the *Academy* magazine in 1907 for which he was paid £300 a year. It is claimed that Bosie had a sexual affair with Romaine Brooks (herself a long-term lover of Natalie Barney in Paris) at about this time ; but this is not admitted to by Bosie in his *Autobiography* and Olive, in any case, seems to have been unaware of this, or unaffected by it. Bosie did however send Brooks a book of his poems inscribed: "We have often told each other imperishable things,"[41] And Brooks herself wrote : "Perhaps [Lord Alfred Douglas] saw in me a dark edition of his own unquenchable youth hiding a like rebellion against the world and its censure. I certainly saw in him a *lapidé*. How could

---

[36] His sister long maintained that he suffered from an overactive thyroid.

[37] Hawkey, op. cit., p. 51.

[38] Quoted in Sewell, op. cit., p. 20.

[39] Sadly, however, he turned out to be psychologically unstable and spent most of his adult life in mental hospitals.

[40] Although, as Olive notes in her diary, she kept receiving letters from people unable to obtain this book. The distribution was completely botched and she had to rebuy most of the unsold copies herself and give them away. Secondhand copies are almost impossible to obtain even today.

[41] Anaïs Nin, *In Favor of the Sensitive Man* (2012), p. 40.

it be otherwise ... a friend of Oscar Wilde. To me the attraction lay precisely in that direction."[42]

Under his editorship the *Academy* became noticeably pro-Catholic, or at least on the Anglo-Catholic wing of the 'High Church' ; it also took up positions on public morality, even to the extent of criticising certain works as fit for censorship. Bosie himself was becoming more and more conservative and self-consciously Christian, while Olive followed him steadily, albeit a few steps behind. She opined in her diary in 1907 that she wanted to shout out "in praise of beauty and so-called 'sin'"[43] and yet the year before, she had already found a local Catholic priest and novelist, Monsignor Bickerstaffe-Drew, a friend of Bosie, "delightful ... clever and interesting" and writes that she almost always likes Catholic priests, who are, she thinks, "as fascinating as the Protestant parsons are dull."[44] In her diary Olive recounts several meetings with this Monsignor, who was evidently a sensitive and interesting man.

In January 1908 the Douglases moved back to London, much to Olive's relief. Her diary shows that her social life took an upward turn. Their large home in Fellows Road, Hampstead, near the idyllic Primrose Hill, combined the best of the advantages of town and country. Olive still had little to do, but she could go for walks on the Hill, and she had more visitors, including admirers. One of them, Ivor Guest, she found rather tedious, perhaps because he had a moustache (something she abhorred in men). But she allowed him to kiss her, even profusely, and enough to make her feel guilty about it. Her days were spent reading, organising the servants and writing letters. In the evenings there were often trips to the theatre. She saw, for example, the Irish plays of J.M. Synge and was introduced to him by the redoubtable

---

[42] quoted in Elliott and Wallace, op. cit, p. 31.

[43] Quoted in Wintermans (2007), op. cit., p. 111.

[44] Olive Custance : *I Desire the Moon : The Diary of Lady Alfred Douglas 1905-1910)* Wintermans, Ed. 2004, p. 35. Monsignor Count Francis Browning Bickerstaffe-Drew was an army chaplain ; he was a renowned literary convert, educated at Pembroke College, Oxford. He wrote many popular novels under the pseudonymn John Aynscough and died in 1928.

Lady Gregory, the celebrated populariser of Irish mythology. Her diary from that time, in which she writes that she liked to be surrounded by the "(if possible *very*) famous" gives the impression that it was a happy time.

In 1909 Bosie fell out horribly with Olive's best childhood friend, Henry Frederick ('Freddie') Walpole Manners-Sutton (a rift only repaired, thanks to Olive, just before the latter's death in 1918). Olive also lost her only sister Cecil. Bosie published his sonnets (including six dedicated to his wife) to wide critical acclaim. The by now poor, depressed and emaciated Pauline Tarn, alias Renée Vivien, who had loved Olive so much, became a Catholic shortly before her death, at 37, in Paris.

In 1910, the couple moved to a smaller, but delightful Queen Anne house in Church Street, near Hampstead Heath (still in London). Life was uneventful.

But the year 1911 turned out to be a bad year for the Douglas family, and the storms were to continue for the next decade. First, Bosie took the plunge and became a Catholic, received into the Church by the same literary priest who had so much impressed his wife, Monsignor Bickerstaffe-Drew. He had been thinking of it for a long time - it had been a constant preoccupation of Wilde and of so many of their circle - so it came as no surprise to those who knew him. Even during the first of the Wilde trials, Wilde had said to him that if he won his action against Queensberry they ought both to be *received into the good old Catholic Church at last*. Bosie had quipped in reply that if he lost the case, they would hardly be welcome anywhere else. Bosie remained faithful to his conversion until his death in 1945.

The conversion, however, was the last straw for Olive's father who broke off friendly relations with Bosie immediately. It was not merely down to a latent dislike for the young man. Colonel Custance had a deep hatred of Catholicism : he had, for example, refused to speak to his only sister after she married a Catholic and became one herself. At the same time, the Douglas' young son Raymond had become a favourite for Olive's father ; he had never had a son of his own and so now he was beginning to fear what he saw as the negative influence of Bosie on the young boy.

In early 1913 Olive left Bosie and returned to live with her father, who had obtained legal custody of Raymond, now aged 10. Olive wrote at the time that she was torn between her husband and her father, heartbroken, and still very much in love with Bosie. She even claimed (to Bosie's mother) that she wished she had the courage to take her own life. Bosie was declared bankrupt and responded to it all by making public criticisms of Colonel Custance that ended in a prosecution for libel ; he was then obliged to make a public apology. Bosie might have won his case but was too confused and overwrought by other litigation at the time, connected (still, after all these years) with Wilde. There followed an attempt by Bosie to recover Raymond : he took him away to the monks of Fort Augustus Abbey School in Scotland, out of the English jurisdiction, but Colonel Custance arranged for him to be brought back, with the boy's agreement. When Bosie discovered that his son had consented, he acquiesced.

The complicated saga of why Bosie failed to defend himself in the libel action brought by Colonel Custance is explained extensively in biographies of Bosie himself ; suffice it to say that it was a time when Bosie was rarely out of the courts, due to different ill-advised libel actions, best described as a cat-fight over the, by now, well-decayed corpse of his former lover, Oscar Wilde. It left Bosie under the probably mistaken apprehension that he had been betrayed by Wilde and by several other former friends. He was full of anger and self pity and so quickly enacted his revenge on Wilde in *Oscar Wilde and Myself* (1914) in which he angrily turned on his old friend. He later came to regret this bitterly and twenty years later told the tale again, retracting most of the hateful things he had written before about Wilde.[45] Not only was he full of anger with the dead Wilde in 1913, but also with his own wife. Her departure was for him a rank betrayal, added to that of his son, who preferred to live with his grandfather. In a poem written, *Before a Crucifix*, he compares

---

[45] In *Oscar Wilde : A Summing-Up* (1940).

them to Judas. But really Olive had no choice; to cut a long story short, the Douglases were stoney broke and Olive's father had offered her financial security in return for the control of their young son, Raymond.

In 1913, after Olive left him, Bosie started living with another woman. Doris Edwards was an American admirer who had come all the way from the States offering to sell her jewels to help him with his debts (mainly connected with his hobby of litigation). He did not take her money but she did become his mistress. At Christmas 1914 a telephone call with Olive brought about a change of heart, and he ended the affair. But the real reunion did not take place until 1918 as the war was ending. For Bosie, 'all the wretchedness of those seven or eight years rolled away'[46]. From then on, the two never permanently lived together again, but neither was there any more infidelity.

There is another important factor that helps to illuminate the vicissitudes of their separation and reconciliation at this time: Olive's conversion to Catholicism. It happened, much to Bosie's surprise, indepently from him; even if one suspects that she might have hoped he would be pleased with her.

Bosie in fact writes to Olive on 17th February 1917[47], expressing his surprise and delight about her wish to be received in the Catholic Church (unfortunately Olive's letters to Bosie from this time have not come to light).

Olive was living at Richmond at the time and she received her instruction in Catholic doctrine from the Marist nuns in that town. She was received by the Rt. Rev. William Francis Brown, Titular Bishop of Pella and Auxiliary Bishop of Southwark; the ceremony took place at St Anne's, Vauxhall some time in 1917.

From a violent letter from Bosie to Olive, dated 8th August 1917[48], it appears that she had already lapsed by that time.

---

[46] Quoted in Wintermans (2007), op. cit., p. 147.

[47] MS Berg Collection, New York Public Library. For this and subsequent pieces of information on this issue, I am indebted to Caspar Wintermans who kindly researched the matter for me.

[48] Ibid.

She was, indeed, a very impulsive woman. However, a letter from Bosie to her, dated 21st November 1918[49], about the time of their reunion after seven or eight years of continual tension, refers to Olive's receiving Holy Communion. Both Olive and Bosie were volatile people, and Olive's interest in Catholicism waxed and waned and was no doubt bound up with her relations with Bosie.

Meanwhile, in 1915, Bosie and Olive had jointly petitioned (unsuccessfully) for the custody of their son. If their petition had been successful it might have helped their marriage. In 1920 Olive took a cottage in Bembridge, near Ryde, on the Isle of Wight and they began to live together again some of the time in Olive's new home. Above the little cottage she had hung a sign: 'Safe haven, after a stormy passage'. In 1925, the unfortunate Raymond wrote to his father and the two were partially reconciled after what had been a twelve-year rift.

During this time on the Isle of Wight Olive was a practising Catholic for a while, perhaps mainly in the summertime, when Bosie was with her. We have seen that Olive converted in 1917 and practised her Catholicism on and off over the next couple of years. Some time after Olive's move to the Isle of Wight, however, she must have taken up the practice of her faith again, because Father Sewell has her down (erroneously) as being received only in 1924, but 'lapsing' in 1927. In any case, the Catholic atmosphere around Ryde at the time was idyllic. The magnificent Catholic Parish Church of St Mary's in Ryde, founded by the Countess of Clare in the mid nineteenth century,[50] was full of Catholic converts and aristocrats, no doubt blessed with the particular good humour and kindliness that comes from living at a popular holiday resort.

Also, since 1901 Ryde had been the home of France's most famous monks, from the Abbey of Solesmes, exiled from France by the anti-Catholic laws. Some of those monks would have been close to Huysmanns and other figures of the Decadent movement in France. They stayed until 1922, but left behind

---

[49] Ibid.

[50] Herself converted by the sight of an elderly man walking a long distance to get to Sunday Mass in bitterly inclement weather.

them a small monastic community with a magnificent new Abbey church which still exists to this day.

In the twenties, the Douglases must have passed some tranquil, happy summers by the sea, in quite a cosmopolitan and Catholic *milieu*.

Through all these twists and turns, Olive continued to help her husband financially. Osbert Lancaster, a good friend of Olive's, claimed that Bosie was 'a deplorable wreck' who had 'treated Olive abominably'. It was not an unreasonable assessment, but Olive loved him, understood him and forgave him. As Evelyn Waugh observed, translating a French proverb, "to understand all is to forgive all."[51] It is perhaps a futile exercise to try to work out who was obliged to forgive the most.

When Olive moved back to London in 1930, Bosie was a frequent visitor. The poet Sir John Betjeman, another faithful friend of Olive's, recalls a Christmas lunch at the Westmoreland Terrace flat in 1930 or 1931 where Bosie was rather silent, listening to a happy and animated Olive. According to Betjeman she was "not at all the sad, inward-looking person her excellent poetry might lead you to believe".[52] Perhaps the fact that she stopped writing her diary and more or less stopped her poetry just before the publication of *The Inn of Dreams* in 1911 is an indication that any tendency to introspection had been overtaken by events. Also, approaching forty, she had grown up. She wrote to a friend :

> I have seen youth go and joy depart,
> But God has given me a merry heart.
> I know that luck fails and love ends,
> But I thank God for my old lovers and new friends.[53]

By the 1930s Bosie had become reconciled both to his past and to his present. In 1931 he published his own critical edition of Shakespeare's Sonnets, dedicated " to Olive " and in

---

[51] In *Brideshead Revisited*.
[52] Sewell, op. cit., p. 27.
[53] To Percy Colson, quoted in his book *What if They Do Mind ?* (1936).

1932 she came to live near him in Hove[54], where, from then on, they saw each other almost every day until Olive's death in 1944, thereby fulfilling the odd wish expressed in her diary as far back as July 1906.

So it was a stormy marriage, but one that held firm for over forty years. There is no doubt that through it all, each of them was the greatest love in the other's life. Even at their most difficult moments Olive, especially, writes to assure Bosie of her undying love.

After 1911 Olive published no more collections of poetry, but in the 1930s, fully reconciled to Bosie, the storms long passed, and grown rather stout[55] in middle age, she did write poems for local newspapers, including patriotic ones during the Second World War. These, along with some fragments in her correspondence and diary, have never been anthologised. In her last years in Hove, Olive had a small circle of interesting friends who met together regularly. These included, apart from her husband, such eccentrics as Marie Stopes, the family planning advocate and Montague Summers, the demonologist and Decadent poet who may well also have been a Catholic priest.[56]

An important theme in all the poetry of the aesthetic movement is the inexorable pull of religious faith. Lurking behind almost every corner is the 'inquiétude de Dieu'.[57] Either there is the gloom and despair of guilt, or there are intimations of joy and light as the poet aspires towards repentance, forgiveness and love. And all of these poets begin in the same place : the quest for beauty and the desire to be fulfilled by being loved in a profound

---

[54] He was a regular, 'eccentric' worshipper at Mass at St Mary Magdalene's, Brighton, where (according to anecdotes of some elderly parishoners relayed by the present incumbent, Fr Ray Blake) the careful parish priest told the altar boys not to accept sweets from him !

[55] Or "jovial and curvy" according to Betjemann (quoted in Sewell, op. cit. p. 27.)

[56] The validity of his orders is, even today, hotly disputed.

[57] 'Worrying about God'

way. This hunger leads them into all sorts of dark alleys, but in the end, the path to Heaven is the most alluring.

It seems worth recalling something that has perhaps slipped rather into oblivion : that almost all the main characters in Wilde's and Douglas' circle of friends became Catholic (even, surprisingly, Bosie's own father[58].) Those who did not, usually thought seriously about it for years. And this, despite the fact that so many of them struggled with the destructive power of transgressive sexuality in their lives. Perhaps *despite* is wrong. Perhaps their sexual torment actually led them to God, or rather such torment was a symptom of their restless hearts, hungering for the infinite. Bosie gives us a clue of this in a poem, composed while he was in Paris and Wilde was in Reading Gaol :

> [Christ] took my soul and bound it
> With cords of iron wire,
> Seven times round He wound it
> With cords of my desire.[59]

Although in this poem he rejects Christ, it is clearly a sorrowful and only temporary rejection. He acknowledges that the adoration of Apollo and the adoration of Christ are coming from the same place : from that restless desire spoken of by St Augustine.[60] In the same year he also asks God to lift his soul "Out of [its] broken past, Where impious feet have trod."[61]

In literary circles, it was a time of incredible sexual licence. Oscar Wilde was only imprisoned because he publicly taunted the justice system into action. It was the working classes who were scandalised by his behaviour ; his own friends and acquaintances had been happy to turn a blind eye. There was no particular social or cultural movement in England or France

---

[58] Joseph Pearce, *Literary Converts*, 1999, p. 17 ; Wintermans (2007), op. cit, p. 94.

[59] *Rejected*, see Wintermans (2007) op. cit.

[60] See St Augustine quotation in the note for the poem *Primrose Hill*, regarding 'Beauty'.

[61] *Ode to my Soul*, see Wintermans (2007) op. cit.

which denounced unorthodox sexual practices nor any which promoted Catholicism. Even the Catholic Church's own voice was fairly discreet in secular society, even if Newman's conversion, and the debates surrounding it, were still within living memory for the older generation. So where did the impetus come from ?

What attracted practically all of these literary people to the Catholic Church, in England and France ? In all probability it was their own consciences and their own *aesthetic sense* that taught them that the round of alcohol, drugs, sex with penniless homosexual prostitutes, pederasty, serial lesbianism, sado-masochism, violence and suicide was not beautiful ; that, in fact, it was a betrayal of their aesthetic ideals. This was the conclusion that so many of these poets and artists freely reached. Of course Olive had never been at heart of the real, epicurean[62] decadence of these men, but she had a strong insight into it, and had flirted with it.

The French Decadent poet Arthur Rimbaud has the key to this, because he would seem to embody in a profound way what Christ said of the woman caught in adultery : " Therefore I tell you, her sins, which are many, are forgiven—for she loved much. But he who is forgiven little, loves little. "[63]

Rimbaud, as a handsome young 16-year-old rebel at the start of his career as a poet, claimed that he needed to descend into the sewer and make himself depraved in order to find his Muse. It was his own personal slant on the philosophy that *one can appreciate the stars most clearly when lying in the gutter*.[64] I am not sure I agree with him, but that is certainly what he did. And yet, at the end of his life, his beauty all spent but the restlessness and the deep longing for *the great love* still there, he discovered that his

---

[62] Epicurus believed that the way to achieve detachment from sensual pleasures was to over-indulge in them.

[63] Luke Ch. 7, v. 47.

[64] "We are all in the gutter, but some of us are looking at the stars" is a line of Lord Darlington in Oscar Wilde's *Lady Windermere's Fan*.

search for the stars – for beauty and truth – had led him back to where he had started as a particularly pious Catholic boy : back to the source of all truth and beauty, God himself. This poet, so influential on the literary figures of the English 1890s died at the age of 37 in 1891, near the beginning of Olive's own odyssey.

"On 10th November, at two o'clock in the afternoon, he was dead," wrote Rimaud's sister Isabelle. The priest, shaken by so much reverence for God, administered the last rites. "*I have never seen such strong faith,*" he said.[65]

Oscar Wilde - and most of the literary figures on both sides of the Channel at the the turn of the century - often suspected, and indeed prayed, that their journeys of love would lead to this same destination. One senses that Wilde's clever witticism (on the lips of the roguish Lord Illingworth in *A Woman of No Importance*) that "every saint has a past and every sinner has a future" was already, in fact, a kind of pious aspiration.

Custance speaks of her youthful self in the first poem in this book, *The Inn of Dreams*, and while still enjoying all the sensual pleasures with her *fairy princes*, she simultaneously hopes or prays that one day, when her youth has left her, *Love* will come by, weeping to see her lonely, and take pity on her. In *The Changeling* she dreams of it too:

> My spirit is a homing dove[66] . . .
> I drain a crystal cup, and fall
> Softly into the arms of Love . . .
> And then the darkness covers all.

---

[65] Quoted by Thomas Bernhard in a lecture published in *Die Zeit*, 14th May 14, 2009 and recently included in an anthology of Bernhard's writings, *Der Wahrheit auf der Spur*. The italics are mine.
[66] Heading for Heaven, no doubt.

And in *The Wings of Fortune*, we see this happen even more definitively, when Christ, coming to her as a beautiful young man[67], throws away his crown of thorns; and like a second Orpheus, he sings his love song to Olive's weary soul and lifts her from death, once more young and radiant.

In her diary (1905-1910) there are some brief but telling references to God and her relationship with Him. Although she finds attendance at a church service 'depressing', she is frightened at night and reads a collection of the sayings of Christ, finding it a 'beautiful book'; another time, she writes simply 'said my prayers'.

The best stories, and the best lives, begin and end with love; or should we say Love with a capital L? For, as Evelyn Waugh observes in *Brideshead Revisited*, "perhaps all our loves are merely hints and symbols; vagabond-language scrawled on gate-posts and paving-stones along the weary road that others have tramped before us; perhaps you and I are types and this sadness which sometimes falls between us springs from disappointment in our search, each straining through and beyond the other, snatching a glimpse now and then of the shadow which turns the corner always a pace or two ahead of us."

In Waugh's novel the ancient Lord Marchmain, after half a lifetime away from the Church he had once embraced, finally makes the sign of the Cross as the priest absolves him. Charles Ryder observes : "Then I knew that the sign I had asked for was not a little thing, not a passing nod of recognition, and a phrase came back to me from my childhood of the veil of the temple being rent from top to bottom."

We must suppose that Bosie had prayed for a similar sign because we know that he often showed a certain Catholic solicitude for his friends at the the time of death. And perhaps it is a kind of happy ending to Olive's story, that five weeks before her passing from this life she expressed deep regret at having left

---

[67] This is my reading of the phrase 'Love the boy'

the practise of her Catholic Faith; and thus began to hope again in its beautiful promises.[68]

She was incoherent at the very end, but slipped away quietly on 12th February 1944[69] holding the hand of her tearful fairy prince.

May she rest in peace.

E.J.K.

Chavagnes en Paillers, France, 21st November 2014.

---

[68] According to Brocard Sewell in his *Olive Custance : Her Life and Work*, 1975, p. 24. I suspect, but cannot prove, that the Parish Priest of St Mary Magdalen's, Brighton, came to administer the last rites. Her funeral was conducted by the local Anglican vicar and she was cremated ; her ashes were scattered at sea many years later.
[69] She died of a brain haemorrhage.

The Inn of Dreams

Sweet Laughter! Sweet Delight!
My heart is like a lighted Inn that waits
Your swift approach . . . and at the open gates
White Beauty stands and listens like a flower.
She has been dreaming of you in the night,
O fairy Princes; and her eyes are bright.
Spur your fleet horses, this is Beauty's hour!
Even as when a golden flame up-curled
Quivers and flickers out in a dark place,
So is it with the flame of Beauty's face~
That torch! that rose! that wonder of the world!
And Love shall weep to see~when he rides by
Years hence (the time shall seem as a bird's flight)~
A lonely Inn beneath a winter sky.
Come now, sweet friends! before the summer die.
Sweet Laughter! Sweet Delight!

Illustration by Aubrey Beardsley

The Kingdom of Heaven

O World that holds me by the wings,
     How shall my soul escape your snares?
So dear are your delightful things,
     So difficult your toils and cares:
That, every way my soul is held
     By bonds of love, and bonds of hate;
With all its heavenly ardours quelled,
     And all its angels desolate . . .

Yet in the heart of every child,
God and the world are reconciled! . . .

Lord Alfred Douglas in 1903 (by George Charles Beresford)

A Dream

I dreamed we walked together, you and I,
Along a white and lonely road, that went
I know not where . . . and we were well content.
Our laughter was untroubled as the sky,
And all our talk was delicate and shy,
Though in that cage of words wild thoughts were pent
Like prisoned birds that some sweet accident
Might yet release to sing again, and fly.
We passed between long lines of poplar trees . . .
Where, summer comrades gay and debonair,
The south wind and the sunlight danced . . . you smiled,
With great glad eyes, as bright as summer seas,
To feel their twinkling fingers in your hair . .
And then you kissed me, quickly, like a child!

Landscape North east of Weston Longville, by Robert Gilbertson.

The Autumn Day

How delicately steps the autumn day
In azure cloak and gown of ashen grey
Over the level country that I love!

With glittering veils of light about her head
And skirts of wide horizons round her spread
White as the white wing-feathers of a dove.

Her feet, a flash of silver on the sea,
Chase silver sails that fly untiringly
Towards the enchanted Islands of the West.

Beautiful Islands, gardens of delight!
That flower at dawn with roses red and white . . .
And flame at sunset gold and amethyst . . .

How delicately steps the autumn day
In azure cloak and gown of ashen grey
Over the level country that I love . . .

And how my heart that all sweet things beguile
Goes laughing with her for a little while . . .
And then turns homeward like a weary dove.

Fra Angelico, detail, *The Last Judgment*.

Angels

When life is difficult, I dream
Of how the angels dance in heaven!
Of how the angels dance and sing
In gardens of eternal spring,
Because their sins have been forgiven . . .
And never more for them shall be
The terrors of mortality!
When life is difficult, I dream
Of how the angels dance in heaven . . .

Illustration from the cover of *The Yellow Book*, Vol. V, by Aubrey Beardsley.

The Changeling

My father was a golden king,
    My mother was a shining queen;
I heard the magic blue-bird sing . . .
    They wrapped me in a mantle green.

They led their winged white horses out,
    We rode and rode till dawn was grey;
We rode with many a song and shout,
    "Over the hills and far away."

They stole the crying human child,
    And left me laughing by the fire;
And that is why my heart is wild,
    And all my life a long desire . . .

The old enchantments hold me still . . .
  And sometimes in a waking trance
I seek again the Fairy Hill,
  The midnight feast, the glittering dance!

The wizard harpers play for me,
  I wear a crown upon my head,
A princess in eternity,
  I dance and revel with the dead . . .

"Vain lies!" I hear the people cry,
  I listen to their weary truth;
Then turn again to fantasy,
  And the untroubled Land of Youth.

I hear the laughter of the kings,
  I see their jewelled flagons gleam . . .
O wine of Life! . . . immortal things
  Move in the splendour of my dream . . .

My spirit is a homing dove . . .
  I drain a crystal cup, and fall
Softly into the arms of Love . . .
  And then the darkness covers all.

A Song Against Care

O Care!
Thou art a cloak too heavy to be borne,
Glittering with tears, and gay with painted lies
(For seldom~seldom art thou stained and torn,
Showing a tattered lining, and the bare
Bruised body of thy wearer); thou art fair
To look at, O thou garment of our pride!
A net of colours, thou dost catch the wise;
He lays aside his wisdom for thy sake . . .
And Beauty hides her loveliness in thee . . .
And after . . . when men know the agony
Of thy great weight of splendour, and would shake
Thee swiftly from their shoulders, cast aside
The burden of thy jewelled bands that break
Their very hearts . . . often it is too late.
They fear the world will mock them and deride
When they are stripped of all their golden state.
But some are brave . . . but some among us dare
Cry out against thy torment and be free!
And I would rather a gay beggar be,
And go in rags for all eternity,
Than that thy clanking pomp should cover me,
O Care! . . .

"Quelque part une Enfance très douce doit mourir"
        Albert Samain

Alas! I do not know on what sad day
My childhood went away . . .
It may have left me softly in the night
    When I was sleeping~dreaming~who can tell?
Perhaps it whispered "wings were made for flight!"
    I only know it never said "farewell" . . .

And so I cannot tell when youth will go
Although I love it so . . .
But like a little amorous girl that clings
    To some fair boy, my spirit all afraid,
While yet she holds youth back by the bright wings,
    Knows he must leave her for some other maid!

Illustration by Aubrey Beardsley

Candle-Light

Frail golden flowers that perish at a breath,
Flickering points of honey-coloured flame,
From sunset gardens of the moon you came,
Pale flowers of passion . . . delicate flowers of death . . .

Blossoms of opal fire that raised on high
Upon a hundred silver stems are seen
Above the brilliant dance, or set between
The brimming wine-cups . . . flowers of revelry!

Roses with amber petals that arise
Out of the purple darkness of the night
To deck the darkened house of Love, to light
The laughing lips, the beautiful glad eyes.

Lilies with violet-coloured hearts that break
In shining clusters round the silent dead,
A diadem of stars at feet and head,
The glory dazzles . . . but they do not wake . . .

O golden flowers the moon goes gathering
In magic gardens of her fairy-land,
While splendid angels of the sunset stand
Watching in flaming circles wing to wing . . .

Frail golden flowers that perish at a breath,
That wither in the hands of light, and die
When bright dawn wakens in a silver sky.
Pale flowers of passion . . . delicate flowers of death.

In the South

I was pale and sad in the South like the olive-trees
That droop their silver heads by the dusty roads,
And are grave and cold and grey in spite of the sun . . .
In the veils of rose and blue that the bright dawn spun
Day wrapped me round in vain!
I longed for the lovers and friends I had left behind,
I longed for the North again.

I was deaf to song, and even to beauty blind,
Blind to the magic woof that summer weaves,
While roses beat their pearl and ruby leaves
Against my window pane . . .
And orange flowers so passionately white,
So richly perfumed, pined for my delight:
Only my faint heart sighed,
In pity when the glory waned and died,
For all that lovely life unsatisfied!

I was pale and sad in the South like the olive-trees
That droop their silver heads by the dusty roads . . .

Spring in the South

Beautiful as some rich embroidery
The valley lies in verdant amplitude,
Great mountains~like old merchants~o'er it brood~
And as a lovely woman languidly
Trailing her long blue robes, so comes the sea
To touch it softly in a wistful mood . . .
The sky forgets her starry multitude,
Seeing how fair mere earthly flowers can be!

Glad country where the wayward feet of Spring,
Moving in mystic dances, bring desire,
New miracles of beauty every day . . .
Where Love and sweet Delight fly wing to wing
Forgetful as in dreams, that bright as fire
So burn the hours of joy as swift away!

Illustration by Aubrey Beardsely.

"I am Weary, let me Sleep"

I am weary, let me sleep
In some great embroidered bed,
With soft pillows for my head.
I am weary, let me sleep . . .
Petals of sweet roses shed
All around a perfumed heap
White as pearls, and ruby red;
Curtains closely drawn to keep
Wings of darkness o'er me spread . . .
I am weary, let me sleep
In some great embroidered bed.
Let me dream that I am dead,
Nevermore to wake and weep
In the future that I dread . . .
For the ways of life are steep . . .
I am weary, let me sleep . . .

Grief

I, that was once so eager for the light,
The vehement pomp and passion of the day,
Am tired at last, and glad to steal away
Across the dusky borders of the night.
The purple darkness now is my delight,
And with great stars my lonely sorrows play,
As still, some proud and tragic princess may
With diamonds make her desolation bright.

Night has become a temple for my tears . . .
The moon a silver shroud for my despair,
And all the golden forests of the spheres
Have showered their splendours on me leaf by leaf
Till men that meet me in the sunlight, stare
To see the shining garment of my grief!

Illustration by Aubrey Beardsley.

Daffodil Dawn

While I slept, and dreamed of you,
Morning, like a princess, came,
All in robe of palest blue:
Stooped and gathered in that hour
From the east a golden flower,
Great and shining flower of flame . . .
Then she hastened on her way
Singing over plain and hill–
While I slept and dreamed of you
Dreams that never can come true . .
Morning at the gates of Day,
Gathered Dawn, the daffodil!

The Virgin with Angels, William-Adolphe Bouguereau, 1900.

Beauty

I saw the face of Beauty~a pale rose
In the gold dusk of her abundant hair . . .
A silken web of dreams and joys~a snare . .
A net of pleasures in a world of woes,
A bright temptation for gay youth that goes
Laughing upon his way without a care!
A shield of light for conquering Love to bear
Stronger than all the swords of all his foes.

O face of Beauty~O white dawn enshrined
In sunrise veils of splendid hair~O star!
Shine on those weary men who sadly wise
But guess thy glory faintly from afar~
Missing the marvel of thy smile~and blind
To the imperial passion in thine eyes!

The Vision

I come from lonely downs and silent woods,
With winter in my heart, a withered world,
A heavy weight of dark and sorrowful things,
And all my dreams spread out their rainbow wings,
And turn again to those bright solitudes
Where Beauty met me in a thousand moods,
And all her shining banners were unfurled . . .
And where I snatched from the sweet hands of Spring
A crystal cup and drank a mystic wine,
And walked alone a secret perfumed way,
And saw the glittering Angels at their play.
And heard the golden birds of Heaven sing,
And woke . . . to find white lilies clustering
And all the emerald wood an empty shrine,
Fragrant with myrrh and frankincense and spice,
And echoing yet the flutes of Paradise . . .

The Dance

Do you remember that day I danced in the woods,
    Under the dancing leaves?
Do you remember the delicate blue of the sky
    And the gold-dust in the air?
And the tawny harvest fields, and the heavy sheaves?
Summer was surely in one of her bravest moods . . .
    And oh, the rare
Swift joy that lifted life to an ecstasy,
That shining day I danced for you, dear, in the woods!

The purple twilight came, and the amber moon . . .
    And the fairies danced with me . . .
And the shy fauns crept from the tangled thicket near,
    And the startled dryads bent,
White and starry-eyed, each from her secret tree,
To watch that mystical dance, to share that heavenly swoon
    That mad, bright banishment. . . .
For we were free in the perfect country, dear,
When purple twilight came and the amber moon . . .

Some day I shall dance again that mystical dance . . .
    I know not when or where!
But the angels shall dance with me, and I shall not be afraid.
    I shall look in their deep eyes . . .
And feel their arms about me, and their kisses in my hair,
And know that time is over, and the desperate ways of chance. . . .
    I shall be very wise,
And glad at last, and the walls of the world shall fade . . .
The day when I dance again that mystical dance.

The Prisoner of God

Once long and long ago I knew delight.
God gave my spirit wings and a glad voice.
I was a bird that sang at dawn and noon,
That sang at starry evening time and night;
Sang at the sun's great golden doors, and furled
Brave wings in the white gardens of the moon;
That sang and soared beyond the dusty world.

Once long and long ago I did rejoice,
But now I am a stone that falls and falls.
A prisoner, cursing the blank prison walls,
Helpless and dumb, with desperate eyes, that see
The terrible beauty of those simple things
My soul disdained when she was proud and free.
And I can only pray: God pity me,
God pity me and give me back my voice!
God pity me and give me back my wings!

The Penitent Magdalene (detail), Guido Reni.

The Storm

What do they hunt to-night, the hounds of the wind?
I think it is joy they hunt, for joy has fled from my heart.
I only remember the hours when I sorrowed or sinned,
I only remember the hours when I stood apart
Lonely and tired, in difficult dreams entranced,
And I forget the days when I loved, and laughed, and danced.

Grey hounds of the wind, I hear your wistful cry,
The cry of unsatisfied hearts hungry for happiness
The house is full of whispering ghosts as you hurry by,
And my soul is heavy and dark with a great distress,
For heaven is far away, and hope is dead;
And the night is a tomb of tears, and despair, and dread.

O hunt no more wild hounds of the wind and rain,
For my soul is afraid of the sound of your hurrying feet,
And surely under the stars a beautiful joy is slain?
Fly! black wings of sorrow . . . wet wings of the night that beat
At the shuttered windows, swiftly fly away,
Before God stoops to gather the golden flower of day.

St Anthony, by Albrecht Dürer.

St. Anthony

THE ENGRAVING BY DÜRER

Dürer has drawn him resting by the way . . .
Has he returned from some far pilgrimage?
Or just come out into the light of day
From a dark hermit's cell? We cannot know . . .
With stooping shoulders, and with head bent low
Over his book~and pointed hood drawn down.
His eager eyes devour the printed page . . .
Regardless of the little lovely town
Rising behind him, with its clustered towers . . .
O Saint, look up! and see how gay and fair
The earth is in its summer-time of flowers,
Look up, and see the world, for God is there . . .
Old dreaming Saint, how many are like you,
Intent upon the dusty book of fate:
Slow to discern the false things from the true!
Yet weary of world clamour and world hate,
And hungering for eternal certainties . . .
Not knowing how close about them heaven lies!

HOW LA BEALE
ISOVD WROTE TO
SIR TRISTRAM

Illustration by Aubrey Beardsley.

Black Butterflies

O words of all my songs . . . black butterflies!
Wild words of all the wayward songs I sing . . .
Called from the tomb of some enchanted past
By that strange sphinx, my soul, they slowly rise
And settle on white pages wing to wing . . .
White pages like flower-petals fluttering
Held spellbound there till some blind hour shall bring
The perfect voice that, delicate and wise,
Shall set them free in fairyland at last!
That garden of all dreams and ecstasies
Where my soul sings through an eternal spring,
Watching alone with enigmatic eyes,
Dark wings on pale flower-petals quivering . . .
O words of all my songs . . . black butterflies!

In Praise of Youth

O delicate youth, thy praises shall be sung
While yet my heart is young . . .
While Life and I, in search of lovely things,
Go out with dancing feet and dreaming eyes,
And find wild Folly, with her rainbow wings,
Sweeter than all the wisdom of the wise.

O delicate Youth, thy praises shall be sung
While yet my heart is young . . .
Thy whiteness, and thy brightness, and the sweet
Flushed softness of thy little restless feet . . .
The tossed and sunny tangle of thy hair,
Thy swiftness, slimness, shyness, simpleness,
That set the old folk sighing for the rare
Red rose of Joy thy careless days possess.

. . . And when at last, with sad, indifferent face,
I walk in narrow pathways patiently;
Forgetful of thy beauty, and thy truth,
Thy ringing laughter, thy rebellious grace . . .
When fair Love turns his face away from me . . .
Then, let me die, O delicate sweet Youth!

Opal Song

Shy and wild . . . shy and wild
To my lovers I have been.
Frank and wayward as a child,
Strange and secret as a queen;
Fain of love, and love beguiled,
Yet afraid of love, I ween!

False and true . . . false and true
Is the woman's heart in me . . .
Fair lost faces that I rue,
Golden friends I laugh to see,
Changing, I come back to you,
Never doubt my loyalty!

Illustration by Aubrey Beardsley.

Gifts

Come near! you are my friend and I will wear
Gems for your sake, and flowers in my hair;
Garments of silver gauze, and cloth of gold . . .
And I will give you power to have and hold,
And passion, and delight and ecstasy.
What will you give to me?

And I will give you, if you will but stay,
The magic mirror of the dawn, where day
Waking, beholds the wonder of her face~
If you will keep me yet in your embrace,
And let me dream of Love's eternity.
What will you give to me?

Yes! I will give you the gold veils of light,
And the dark spangled curtains of the night . . .
And I will give you as a flower unfurled,
The proud and marvellous beauty of the world,
And all the wild, white horses of the sea.
What will you give to me? . . .

Primrose Hill

Wild heart in me that frets and grieves,
Imprisoned here against your will . . .
Sad heart that dreams of rainbow wings
See! I have found some golden things!
The poplar trees on Primrose Hill
With all their shining play of leaves . . .

Proud London like a painted Queen,
Whose crown is heavy on her head . . .
City of sorrow and desire,
Under a sky of opal fire,
Amber and amethyst and red . . .
And how divine the day has been!
For every dawn God builds again
This world of beauty and of pain . . .

Wild heart that hungers for delight,
Imprisoned here against your will;
Sad heart, so eager to be gay!
Loving earth's lovely things . . . the play
Of wind and leaves on Primrose Hill . . .
Or London dreaming of the night . . .
Adventurous heart, on beauty bent,
That only Heaven could quite content!

A Morning Song

You saw my window open wide,
And woke me early, sister day!
You came in all your lovely pride,
With laughing looks that I adore,
With wings of blue and grey . . .
With sunshine skirts that swept the floor,
With songs to drive night's dreams away,
You called me out to play.
And so I took you by the hand,
And found the way to fairyland . . .
With such impatient feet I climb
The ladders of delight!
For well I know that ruthless time
Turns morning moods to tears and night.

The Wings of Fortune

Fair fortune you are wild and coy,
Fickle, mysterious, and shy . . .
And so we lost you, Love and I!
And now, at last, because we find
Your golden footprints, Love the boy,
Dreams you are near . . . but Love is blind!
Yet, surely Sorrow's arms unwind

From this tired heart, and dark distress
Fades softly . . . softly from the world:
And in Hope's silver sky unfurled,
I see the banners of delight!
And the grey heaven of life grows bright
With the red dawn of happiness . . .
As with a laughing look Love flings
His heavy crown of thorns away . . .
Fair fortune, you are wild and coy,
And ah! I fear you will not stay.
But Love has caught you by the wings
And radiant as Eurydice
By her brave poet's song set free,
I rush into the arms of joy!

Shadow-Nets

When I was wandering on the Downs to-day
I saw the pine-woods sleeping in the sun . . .
For they were tired of weaving shadow-nets~
Weaving all day in vain . . . in vain . . . in vain . . .
Pale phantom nets to snare the golden sun!
And then I thought of how the poets weave
With shadowy words their cunning nets of song,
Hoping to catch, at last, a shining dream!

Peacocks. A Mood

In Gorgeous plumage, azure, gold and green,
They trample the pale flowers, and their shrill cry
Troubles the garden's bright tranquillity!
Proud birds of Beauty, splendid and serene,
Spreading their brilliant fans, screen after screen
Of burnished sapphire, gemmed with mimic suns~
Strange magic eyes, that, so the legend runs,
Will bring misfortune to this fair demesne . . .

And my gay youth, that, vain and debonair,
Sits in the sunshine~tired at last of play
(A child, that finds the morning all too long),
Tempts with its beauty that disastrous day
When in the gathering darkness of despair
Death shall strike dumb the laughing mouth of song.

The death of Hyacinthus, by Jean Broc, 1801.

Hyacinthus

Fair boy, how gay the morning must have seemed
Before the fatal game that murdered thee!
Of such a dawn my wistful heart has dreamed:
Surely I too have lived in Arcady
When Spring, lap-full of roses, ran to meet
White Aphrodite risen from the sea . . .

Perchance I saw thee then, so glad and fleet;
Hasten to greet Apollo, stoop to bind
The gold and jewelled sandals on his feet,
While he so radiant, so divinely kind,
Lured thee with honeyed words to be his friend,
All heedless of thy fate, for Love is blind.

For Love is blind and cruel, and the end
Of every joy is sorrow and distress.
And when immortal creatures lightly bend
To kiss the lips of simple loveliness,
Swords are unsheathed in silence, and clouds rise,
Some God is jealous of the mute caress . . .

But who shall mourn thy death~ah, not the wise?
Better to perish in thy happiest hour,
To close in sight of beauty thy dark eyes,
And, dying so, be changed into a flower,
Than that the stealthy and relentless years
Should steal that grace which was thy only dower.

And bring thee in return dull cares and tears,
And difficult days and sickness and despair . . .
O, not for thee the griefs and sordid fears
That, like a burden, trembling age must bear;
Slain in thy youth, by the sweet hands of Love,
Thou shalt remain for ever young and fair . . .

Hylas and the Nymphs, by John William Waterhouse, 1896. (Detail)

Hylas

Dark boy, how radiantly you went to meet
Your mystic doom . . . what colours in the sky!
As though that cup of beauty the gods hold
Brimmed over on a world in ecstasy . . .
What silver flutes charmed all the forest ways . . .
How the green shimmered, jewelled thick with flowers,
And how the sun was like a globe of gold . . .
Yet you but thought to chase the perfect hours
Down that white road of wonder and delight,
The highway of your dreams, and heedlessly
You crushed the violets with your slim brown feet,
And whistled low, and sang a careless song . . .
Because your life was full of lovely days,
Because your life was delicate and sweet . . .
O youth and dawn . . . you dreamed not of the night . . .
O life and laughter . . . but the night is long . . .

Blue Flowers

I go to gather in the woods for you
The wild flowers that are blue . . .
Petals to match the colour of your eyes!

None but blue blossoms will I take, yet see
How sweetly tempting me
The fruit trees swing their scented treasuries.

And how the buttercups and daisies dance
To meet my dazzled glance!
But gold and silver, Sweet, are naught to you.

And so let others rob God's gardens . . . shake
The stars down for your sake~
I bring you but the wild flowers that are blue!

Madrigal

Rare garden where my heart goes gathering
Many a lovely and delightful thing,
Pale roses of your body and the fair
Unrivalled yellow blossoms of your hair!

Tall lilies of your gay and careless grace,
And O the wistful flower of your face!
And all the soft and starry mysteries
Of those divine forget-me-nots, your eyes . . .

O come, fair Love, before the flowers fade,
And bless this garden that the gods have made . . .
Rare garden where my heart goes gathering
Many a lovely and delightful thing . . .

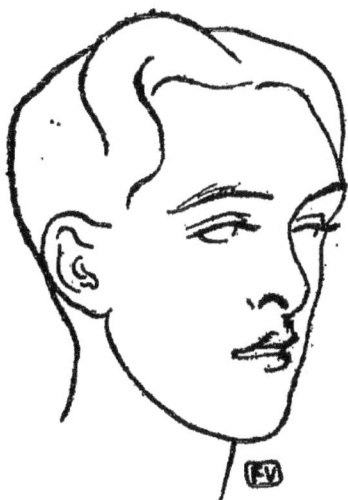

Lord Alfred Douglas by Félix Valloton
from *La Revue blanche*, 1896.

Endymion by George Frederick Watts, 1872.

Endymion

Your hair was like a honey-coloured flame
Seen through a veil of silver when you came
And took me in your arms that winter night . . .
The moonlight, amorous of your golden hair,
Toyed with it softly, as a woman might
With some bright treasure, delicate and rare.

O, young Endymion, risen from the dead,
Born once again to beauty, O bright head!
The moon stoops low to kiss you, as of old;
Stoops graciously from her great throne of pearl,
With outstretched arms mysterious and cold . . .
But you have left her for a mortal girl.

Dance Song

O hide your passion from the moon.
When young and slender she appears
In shining gown and silver shoon . . .
And, all her path with stars impearled,
She dances round the darkened world.

O hide your sorrows from the sun . . .
The sun should never see your tears!
Weep, if you will, when day is done . . .
But laugh and sing and clap your hands
While yet the sun in heaven stands.

William Bouguereau. *La jeunesse de Bacchus.* (1884)

John Gray, about 1890.

A Memory

O how I loved you when we met
For that one moment of the day!
Yes, loved you desperately, and yet
Could scarcely find a word to say~
No wonder that you looked and smiled
As though upon some timid child.
You never guessed, how could you guess
That I adored your loveliness!

You never saw the prisoned soul
Behind the windows of my eyes,
Frantic to break from fate's control
And charm you with her flatteries . . .
And show you, your cold heart to move,
The shining treasure of her love,
And worship in a long embrace,
The reckless beauty of your face!

You never knew . . . and the dream died
A broken rose beneath your feet . . .
You went your way . . . the world is wide
And I forgot, for youth is sweet . . .
Yet when at night I lie awake,
My heart is sad for a dream's sake,
And I remember and regret . . .
O how I loved you when we met!

Olive Custance, about 1910.

The Photograph

O Beauty, what is this?
A shadow of your face . . .
Where is the wild flower grace
That Love is wont to kiss?

Where is the bird that brings
To your untroubled eyes
The blue of fairy skies,
The flash of fairy wings? . . .

O wild bird of delight,
That no white hand may hold,
Or fairest cage of gold . . .
For who would stay its flight?

The song-bird of your voice
Whose magic song Love hears,
Trembling behind your tears,
Trilling when you rejoice . . .

O Beauty, what is this?
The shadow of a rose . . .
A little ghost that goes
Oblivious of Love's kiss.

Only a shadow . . . yet
It may, in some dark hour
Recall the living flower . . .
If haply Love forget.

Guido Reni's St. Sebastian

St. Sebastian

So beautiful in all thine agony!
So radiant in thine infinite despair . . .
Oh, delicate mouth, brave eyes, and curled bright hair . . .
Oh, lovely body lashed to the rough tree:
What brutal fools were those that gave to thee
Red roses of thine outraged blood to wear,
Laughed at thy bitter pain and loathed the fair
Bruised flower of thy victorious purity?

Marvellous Beauty . . . target of the world,
How all Love's arrows seek thy joy, Oh Sweet!
And wound the white perfection of thy youth!
How all the poisoned spears of hate are hurled
Against thy sorrow when thou darest to meet
With martyrdom men's mockery of the truth!

The Magic Mirrors

In the dim mirrors of imagination,
I watch the silent dancing of my soul . . .
I watch her as she dances with my dreams . . .
See how she takes innumerable disguises,
And hides her beauty behind many masks,
And how, sometimes, she seems to laugh and sing,
. . . And weep . . . and call upon the unknown Gods . . .
But not one mirror has betrayed her voice,
Or shown to me the secret of her face . . .
O silent dance of sorrow and delight,
My heart grown tired with watching, turns away,
To make perhaps a little passionate song
Out of the shadows of immortal things . . .

AVE ATQVE VALE

AVBREY BEARDSLEY.

AB.

Notes on the poems

Dedication by the Comtesse de Noailles (p. vi)

Here follows a translation, by the present editor :

« I WRITE FOR THE DAY WHEN I'LL NO LONGER BE »

I write for the day when I'll no longer be,
So they'll know how fresh air and fun pleased me,
That my book might future folks remind
That I loved life and was the happy kind.

Watching the work of the fields and the home
And the seasons' turn, where'er I roam
Water and earth and flame, for my part
Seem nowhere more fair than in my own heart.

What I've seen and felt I have honestly told
With a heart for which truth was not too bold
And I've had this desire, whispered by love's breath :
To be sometimes loved still even after my death.

And that some young man who then reads what I write,
In a trice thoughts of living wives put to flight,
Moved, troubled, surprised by a heart long dead
Will then welcome *me* in his dear soul instead.

The Inn of Dreams (p. 1)

In correspondence, the author called her husband, Lord Alfred Douglas, 'the fairy prince'. Custance sees herself as waiting and providing comfort, light and warmth and perhaps sensual delights for a weary traveller : 'My heart is like a lighted Inn'. No doubt, after the death of Wilde (in 1900) and the years of stress and anguish in Douglas' relationship with him, this was what her love felt like for him. They married in March 1902.

She also encourages him : he is still young and beautiful, and so is she : 'this is Beauty's hour' ... 'before the summer die'. In later poems *Beauty* can seem to refer either to the poet and her youthful self or to a benign feminine spirit (perhaps the Virgin Mary) and Love refers several time to Christ.

Beauty is also seen as something good in itself, but which can in fact can lead on either to sadness and destuction, or to the ultimate Beauty which is God Himself. (See quotation from St Augustine in the note on *Primrose Hill*.) One reading, then, of this poem could be almost as an invitation to sin while young, acknowledging that it could make true *Love* (Christ, or at least a mature Christian conscience) weep when later she feels guilt for sin ; sexual sin, in this context, seems almost a duty for the young and beautiful : "gather ye rosebuds while ye may ".

My personal opinion is that the plural in 'fairy Princes' is a discreet reference to Father John Gray. (See my note on the poem 'A Memory').

The Kingdom of Heaven (p. 3)

"Truly I say to you, unless you are converted and become like children, you will not enter the kingdom of heaven." Matthew 18: 3.

Custance expresses despair that life is full of irresistible temptations and sufferings, while the undeniable attraction of God ('heavenly ardours') is obscured by wordly concerns. Beautiful people ('angels') seem to us to eternal truths, and yet they often seem 'desolate'. Or perhaps the reference to angels is more about her prayers falling on deaf ears in Heaven. The opening lines are especially poignant : it is our desire of beauty that should make us find God, and yet 'the world' grasps our wings so that we cannot fly. We are trapped by its 'snares'.

But in the beautiful face of a child, all of these tensions find resolution, as Christ suggests in Matthew Ch. 18. Custance had her first and only child, Raymond, in November 1902.

A Dream (p. 5)
This sonnet seems to speak of the courtship of Douglas and Custance. He is fascinated by her, but shy. It is his first intimate relationship with a woman. The 'sweet accident' of meeting Custance releases 'the prisoned birds' of his love for her, as they walk past his old 'summer comrades', the memory of whom still gives him a frisson. His kiss, perhaps the first of its kind, is like that 'of a child', shaken and surprised ('quickly') by discovery.

The *south wind*, Notus, announces the end of summer. But in Greek mythology the west wind (Zephyr) and the sun (Apollo) were both in love with the boy Hylas. Perhaps an allusion to this was in fact intended. First appeared 1905 in *The Blue Bird*.

The Autumn Day (p. 7)
See also *A Morning Song* where the day is a lady dressed in blue and grey ; and also *Daffodil Dawn* where it is a lady in blue.

The 'level country' is presumably the flat Norfolk countryside around the Custance family estate at Weston Longville. 'Islands of the West' : somewhat obscure, but perhaps a reference to Lyonesse, the mythical isle that sank into the sea near Cornwall. In Tennyson's *Idylls of the King* it is the place of the last battle between King Arthur and Mordred. It could also be a reference to the *Land of Youth*, mentioned elsewhere in these poems. First appeared in *The Blue Bird*, 1905.

Angels (p. 9)
Heavenly bliss has often been represented by the dance of the angels, commonly portrayed on church ceilings and in Medieval and Renaissance paintings. A well known example is the dance of

the angels and the blessed in Fra Angelico's 'Last Judgement' (pictured beside the poem). St Clement of Alexandria claimed that in Heaven, the just would dance with the angels in the joy of the fullness of truth and the vision of God.

In Medieval hymnology there are many references to the ring dance of angels or of the virgins. With the exception of the sphere of Saturn, which was the sphere of contemplation, the spheres in Dante's Paradise are full of light, music and dance. In the sphere of the sun, the souls of the wise and learned perform a ring dance that encircles Dante and Beatrice. The light, harmony and bliss of heaven radiated from this dance of the souls. So the notion of the angelic dance is firmly rooted not just in fine art and spirtuality, but also in literature.

Custance knew the difference between angels and saints and is really talking about the latter here; but the word 'angel' seems to conjure up the idea of carefree joy and lightness, whereas we somehow wrongly associate the saints only with penance and suffering.

The Changeling (p. 10)
A changeling, in (mainly Celtic) mythology was a fairy child substituted for a human baby soon after its birth. Children with strange or amoral behaviour were sometimes suspected of being changelings. A part of Custance clings to carefree existence of youth.

'Over the hills and far away' is a line in several childrens' rhymes and folk songs. It suggests the freedom and dreaminess of childhood.

In Irish mythology and folklore, Tír na nÓg ("Land of the Young") or Tír na hÓige ("Land of Youth") is one of the names for the Otherworld, or perhaps for a part of it. It is depicted as a supernatural realm of everlasting youth, beauty, health, abundance and joy. Its inhabitants are the Tuath Dé ("people of the gods"), the gods of pre-Christian Ireland, although in later lore they are called simply 'the little people' or the fairies. Various ancient Irish heroes visit Tír na nÓg after a voyage or an invitation from one of its residents. They reach it by entering ancient burial mounds or caves, or by going under water or across the sea. Such accounts occur also in much later fairy tales. Afterwards, such people are afflicted with a longing to return to the fairy kingdom and some are allowed to do so, rather like Tolkien's Bilbo Baggins who ends his days in the Elven kingdom of Rivendell.

Tír na nÓg is best known from the tale of Oisín and Niamh. In the tale, Oisín (a human hero) and Niamh (a woman of the Otherworld) fall in love. She brings him to Tír na nÓg on a magical horse that can travel over water. After spending what seems to be three years there, Oisín becomes homesick and wants to return to Ireland. Niamh reluctantly lets him return on the magical horse, but warns him never to touch the ground. When he returns, he finds that 300 years have passed in Ireland. Oisín falls from the horse. He instantly becomes elderly, as the years catch up with him, and he quickly dies of old age.

'My spirit is a homing dove' : with her marriage to Douglas, she has, as it were, attained to the Holy Grail of her bohemian quest for love. She no longer, in fact, seeks the Fairy Kingdom of pure sensuality, even if the 'old enchantments' still have a fascination, and 'sometimes in a waking trance' she reaches out to them. When she is united to him sexuallly in 'the arms of Love' she is able to forget that 'long desire', as 'darkness covers all.'

It is worth noting that in at least one other poem, Love represents Christ. Another equally fair reading of the poem is that as that her spirit, the homing dove, is inexorably seeking out Heaven and that once she has taken the mystic Communion wine from the 'crystal cup', she can sleep safely in the arms of Christ. Probably, both meanings are present at once. The spiritual battle between fairyland and Heaven is expressed in the phrase "weary truth", almost an oxymoron; she knows that in the end she must give in to Christ.

A Song Against Care (p. 12)
The message seems to be that those who seem to have happy and glamorous lives are in fact full of sadness. Marrying Douglas was a

financial risk because he had been cut out of his father's inheritance. But she has followed her heart and found happiness, although, in the future, there were to be serious difficulties in the marriage. At the time of Douglas' conversion to Catholicism in 1911 (the year these poems were published) she admired his courage.

"Quelque part une Enfance très douce doit mourir" (p. 13)
Albert Victor Samain (April 3, 1858 – August 18, 1900) was a French poet and writer of the Symbolist school. Born in Lille, of Flemish stock, he came from a poor family and in his youth had to sacrifice his education and ambitions to look after his sick mother, although he taught himself Latin and Greek and was widely read. He moved to Paris in around 1880, where his poetry won him a following and he began mixing with avant-garde literary society, and began publicly reciting his poems at Le Chat Noir. His poems were influenced by those of Baudelaire and Verlaine.

Samain published three volumes of verse: *Le jardin de l'infante* (1893), which made him famous; *Aux flancs du vase* (1898) and *Le Chariot d'or* (1901). His poetic drama *Polyphème* was set to music by Jean Cras. Samain died of tuberculosis in 1901. Custance would have read his poetry in French because translations were not readily available before 1912.

Symbolism is a movement in art and litterature that rejected realism and used symbols to evoke ideas and emotions. It is often characterised by what has been called 'l'inquiétude de Dieu' (an obsession or anxiety about God), a sense of sadness, and a weariness about human sexuality, which Samain called 'fruit de mort à l'arbre de vie' ("fruit of death upon the tree of life"). Jethro Bithell, who translated all of the symbolists, wrote of "a certain characteristic ache" in Samain's poetry.

In Samain's poetry, then, a mood is created by the presentation of various striking but not necessarily connected images. The image of a sweet, little girl dying is the most striking in the poem.

Here is the orginal of his poem *Soir*, from which Custance quotes :

Le Séraphin des soirs passe le long des fleurs...
La Dame-aux-Songes chante à l'orgue de l'église ;
Et le ciel, où la fin du jour se subtilise,
Prolonge une agonie exquise de couleurs.

Le Séraphin des soirs passe le long des coeurs...
Les vierges au balcon boivent l'amour des brises ;
Et sur les fleurs et sur les vierges indécises
Il neige lentement d'adorables pâleurs.

Toute rose au jardin s'incline, lente et lasse,
Et l'âme de Schumann errante par l'espace
Semble dire une peine impossible à guérir...
Quelque part une enfant très douce doit mourir...
O mon âme, mets un signet au livre d'heures,
L'Ange va recueillir le rêve que tu pleures.

Translation by Jethro Bithell (1912) :

THE seraph of the eve past flower-beds strays ...
The subtle colours of the sunset die
An exquisite death, long lingering in the sky;
The Lady of Reveries the Church organ plays.

Past hearts the seraph of the evening goes ...
The virgins drink love on the zephyr's wing;
And on the flowers and virgins opening
Adorable paleness gradually snows.

The roses bow their heads as night grows darker;

The soul of Schumann wandering through space
A pain incurable seems to be sighing ...
Somewhere a little baby must be dying ...
My soul, put in the breviary a marker,
The Angel takes the tears from thy dream's face.

Custance misquotes or misremembers the original in her
quotation from Samain. Instead of a 'very sweet little girl dying',
she speaks of her own *childhood dying*. I think she means more *my
childhood has to die*, rather than my *childhood must be dying*. The
French is ambiguous.

Candle-Light (p. 14)
Very much a symbolist poem, where a series of colours, images
and moods are presented in an enigmatic way.

   According to Karl Beckson (*Aesthetes and Decadents of the
1890's*, 1966) this poem is evidence of Custance's classification as
a Decadent. It displays 'the weariness of the Decadent ... his mark
of sophistication.'

   There does perhaps seem to be a suggestion that this is about
beautiful girls and all their sensuality. Or it could be that these
delicate flowers are the sensuality of impure fantasies that
dissipate with the arrival of the dawn and the awakening of the
conscience. Perhaps the contrast of gold and rose (suggesting
richness, beauty), white (purity) and violet (penance and sorrow) is
deliberate. All of these are Catholic liturgical colours, which
themselves draw their meaning from an ancient common
symbolical language. They also belong to the typical colour palette
of Decadent poetry. It is very reminiscent of Arthur Samain's
poem quoted in the note to the previous poem "Quelque part une
Enfance très douce doit mourir". The poem was first published in
The Blue Bird, 1905.

In the South (p. 15)

Keats exclaims "O for a beaker full of the warm South !" in his 'Ode to a Nightingale'. Yet a certain *nostalgie* for the North goes back even to the Greeks, who believed in a northern paradise called *Hyperborea* where men were more noble and pure. The English are sometimes torn between North and South, geographically, culturally and even theologically. Here, also, the poet believes she ought to enjoy the summer sun of the South, but simply feels cut off from what is comfortingly familiar back in England. Is there also in this something of the anguish of someone drawn to mediterranean culture, its traditions and its spirituality (Catholicism) but held back from enjoying it because of 'lovers and friends' back home ? First appeared in *The Blue Bird*, 1905.

Spring in the South (p. 16)

In contrast to the previous poem, here the poet is able to reconnect with the joy of created things, and leave off her melancholy. It is a coming down to earth : the infinity of stars is too far off ; far better the joyful beauty of flowers in the sunshine.

"I am Weary, let me Sleep" (p. 17)

This poem, and the one that follows it, see Custance plunged into sadness and despair, tired of suffering.

Grief (p. 18)

First published in 1905, in *The Blue Bird*. Purple, the colour of penance in Christian symbolism, surrounds her *temple* of tears. And her prayers reach heaven, even playing with 'with great stars' which do actually bring her comfort and make 'her desolation bright'. And through her suffering, the subject of the poem (presumably its author) is being transformed by mysterious heavenly graces ('the spheres'), *even if it still hurts*. Her friends can see that she is transfigured by this spiritual awakening that has been bought at the price of all her weary suffering. The poem begins with the poetess fleeing the light, and worldly 'pomp', only to end with her radiating light, almost despite herself.

Daffodil Dawn (p. 19)

It is unclear to whom the poem, first published in 1905 (in *The Blue Bird*), is addressed ; perhaps to her husband, perhaps to another man or woman for whom she feels a sexual desire to which she does not wish to succomb, because of her marriage commitment to Douglas and because of her moral principles. The sexual fantasies of dreams which the poetess at this time perhaps already had begun to think of as 'impure thoughts' disappear with the coming of the day.   Perhaps the princess, draped in blue, is a reference to the Virgin Mary as well as to the dawning light. And perhaps the golden, fiery daffodil from the east is a spiritual gift to replace those 'dreams that can never come true'.

Beauty (p. 21)

This poem, I am convinced, is placed deliberately after the one before it (*Daffodil Dawn*). *Beauty* is not just a celebration of feminine beauty. It takes the personification of the Dawn a step further : it is a delicate suggestion of the attractive power of the Virgin Mary. With the Catholic conversion of her husband, and with already nascent Catholic sympathies of her own, this must have been something Olive and Bosie had talked about together.

It is easy to fall into the trap of thinking the first stanza is speaking of the deceptive 'snare' of worldly beauty, waiting to trap us with is suffering and pain. We have certainly encounteed this in other poems. But no, this would run completely counter to the prayer-like second stanza. The sense of the first stanza is surely that celestial beauty can in fact be every bit as seductive as that of the the world, the flesh and the devil. This is all about a 'star' (Custance's code for the philosophical or spiritual realm) who is at once terrifyingly seductive, martial ('imperial'), glorious and kind (the 'smile').

Cf. Song of Songs 6 : 10. "Who is she that cometh forth as the morning rising, fair as the moon, bright as the sun, terrible as an army set in battle array? " (Applied by the Catholic liturgy to the Virgin Mary).

Regarding the 'star', the Virgin Mary, of course, is called *Star of the Sea* and *Star of the Morning*, in Catholic mystical poems and hymns.

The Vision (p. 22)

This poem continues the themes of the previous two : Wordsworthian encounters with nature, lead to a series of more and more explicit meditations on Christian spirituality. First, capitalised 'Beauty', and the 'Spring' (the Virgin ?), ' a crystal cup ... of mystic wine' (intimation of Holy Communion and the Blood of Christ ?), 'Angels at play', 'Heaven' ... and then, before it becomes too direct and obvious, our poetess awakes. But her benevolent feminine muse has left 'white lilies' (the traditional sign of the Virgin Mary's purity) and lastly 'myrrh and frankincense' (two of the three gifts left with Mary by the three Wise Men for the baby Jesus. The other gift, gold, has already been given to the poetess in the poem *Daffodil Dawn*.) The wood has become a shrine ... even if it is empty. Yet something still calls gently towards Faith : 'echoing yet the flutes of Paradise.' We are made to wonder : was it really just a dream ? The poem's title suggests something more.

The Dance (p. 23)

The poetess remembers the carefree sensuality and energy of her 'pagan' youth, peopled with fauns and dryads, as if in the court of the ancient Pan. In its love, and beauty and joy, it was like a foretaste of Heaven, where she hopes to dance again, *wise* and *glad*, after death. (See previous notes for the poems 'Land of Youth' and 'Changeling').

The Prisoner of God (p. 24)

It is as if all the previous poems have been a preparation for this one. This is not metaphor, this is not a conceit, nor an example of poetic licence. This is a prayer. Now, the message is clear. It is a direct plea to God and a humble confession of past folly. The poetess mourns her lost innocence and wants to recover the simplicity of a child. She wants to rediscover joy and purity and peace. Her *wings* are perhaps her playful, optimistic self, or even her spiritual side ; her *voice* is perhaps her poetic muse. Perhaps also she sees the storms gathering in her own life.

The Storm (p. 25)

This is a lucid, but hopeful description of how a Christian can feel oppressed by the memories of past sins and sufferings and forget what it feels like to be joyful. The *hope* is in the extremely determined prayer for deliverance and the assurance that God will give her consolation with the new day. The image for this consolation is that of the gift of a golden flower gathered at dawn (as in *Daffodil Dawn*.)

St. Anthony (p. 27)

Somehow the storm has lifted. We have here a complete change of mood. This is no longer the voice of a lost soul ! With what seems like a newfound and confident faith, our poetess calls stuffy Christians to engage with the world, to experience the beauty of nature and of man himself. The Kingdom of Heaven starts here, after all.

Black Butterflies (p. 29)

A charming poem, reminiscent of the opening *Dedication* by the Comtesse de Noailles. Perhaps, dear Reader, yours is the 'perfect voice' that will set the butterflies (the words of these poems) free. First published in *The Blue Bird*, 1905.

In Praise of Youth (p. 30)

'Then, let me die' : not because she wants to die, but because, if
we want to live well, we should all remain 'young at heart' until
we die.

Opal Song (p. 31)

Opal is a stone which seems to contain many different colours.
Custance had 'a strange passion' for opals, and liked 'to be called,
and to call herself, Opal', according to Father Brocard Sewell (in
his *Life* of the poet). The shifting colours of the opal perhaps
mirror the capricious nature of the poet's own erotic feelings, or
of her peersonality in general. This poem first appeared in *Opals*,
published in 1897.

Gifts (p. 32)

'To have and to hold' is in the text of the marriage service, but
perhaps it is rather Heaven that is speaking to man ; yet again, in
the guise of a woman.

Primrose Hill (p. 33)

Primrose Hill is a hill on the northern side of Regent's Park in
London, and also the name given to the surrounding district. The
hill has a clear view of central London to the south-east, as well as
Belsize Park and Hampstead to the north. In the nineteenth
century terraces of houses were built nearby for wealthy families.
It has the aspect of a little village, very near the heart of London.
The Douglases moved to 39 Fellows Road, Hampstead, a short
walk from the hill, in about 1907 when Bosie took up editorship
of *The Academy*. A diary entry in August 1908 has Olive musing
on the beauty of the scene and resolving to 'make a poem'.

    Sitting on the hill, our poet is surprised to find some respite
from London life. The poem is full of, by now, familiar themes :
the poet's own 'wild heart', the search for 'golden things', her love

of nature, the burden of care, God's gift of a golden new beginning every day.

Most striking of all is the line 'Sad heart, so eager to be gay !' which so poignantly sums up the poet's quest. The last couplet recalls St Augustine, whom Custance must by now have read and taken to heart :

"Late have I loved thee, O Beauty ever ancient, ever new, late have I loved thee! Thou wert within me, but I was outside, and it was there that I searched for thee. In my unloveliness I plunged into the lovely things which thou didst create. Thou wert with me, but I was not with thee. Created things kept me from thee; yet if they had not been in thee they would have not been at all. Thou didst call, thou didst shout, and thou didst break through my deafness. Thou didst flash and shine, and didst dispel my blindness. Thou didst breathe thy fragrance on me; I drew in breath and now I pant for thee. I have tasted thee, now I hunger and thirst for more. Thou didst touch me, and I burned for thy peace ... Thou hast made us for thyself, O Lord, and our heart is restless until it rests in thee." (St Augustine, *Confessions*).

A Morning Song (p. 34)
One observes again the image of the new dawn heralded by a beautiful, kind lady in blue (and this time, grey), which is present in several of the poems. It could be about romantic love, about the Virgin Mary, about the call of the countryside, about a kind of sweet and childish escapism, or being alone with one's happy dreams, or about the onset of middle age. Or it could be about all these things at once. One imagines, as this deals with themes that are so strongly recurrent, that perhaps when she slept alone at night the poet sometimes may have suffered from night terrors or, at least, a deep sadness and loneliness.

The Wings of Fortune (p. 35)
For 'Fortune', read the bohemian, spontaneous lifestyle of the poet's youth and the joy it can bring. For Love, understand the

person of Christ who no longer seems so forbidding because he 'throws His heavy crown of thorns away' and replaces the sorrow of the crucifixion with the joy of his Resurrection and His individual loving care for each soul.

In Greek mythology, Eurydice was an oak nymph or one of the daughters of Apollo (the god of light). She was the wife of Orpheus, who tried to bring her back from the dead with his enchanting love songs.

The poet's old self has died, abandoned by fair Fortune. But Love, in the person of Christ, has brought her back from sorrowful death with his personal and loving approach to her.

The Feast of the Triumph of the Holy Cross which the Catholic and Orthodox Churches celebrate in September, features this 6th century hymn, which seems to paint the same sort of image of a sky alive with a red dawn of bright banners, in the wake of the Passion and resurrection of Christ :

The royal banners forward go,
 the cross shines forth in mystic glow;
 where he in flesh, our flesh who made,
 our sentence bore, our ransom paid.

Where deep for us the spear was dyed,
 life's torrent rushing from his side,
 to wash us in that precious flood,
 where mingled water flowed, and blood.

When our poet exclaims 'Fair Fortune, you are wild and coy, And ah ! I fear you will not stay' she is wistfully bidding farewell to her old life. The Love which has caught her (or her Fortune) by the wings (for 'wings', she means her desire, her ache, her yearning, her fairy nostalgia, her spiritual self, ...) is no longer the old, capricious fairy love, but Christ, who is Love itself.

The title seems also to suggest that she cannot, as it were, believe her luck ; also that she sees her old life as having lent her the wings to fly high enough to find the real life of the spirit.

Shadow-Nets (p. 36)

She need not fret. Our poet catches the shining dream well enough !

Peacocks. A Mood (p. 37)

'Strange magic eyes ... will bring misfortune' : having peacock feathers in the house was often thought to bring bad luck. Argus, in Greek mythology, who had 100 eyes.

After being discovered by the King of Egypt to be guilty of an act of deception, he was turned into a peacock and his eyes became the 'eyes' on a peacock's feather. Some traditions hold that the eyes themselves bring the bad luck, rather like the 'evil eye'. The peacock is a symbol of Pride, one of the Seven Deadly Sins. Peacock feathers were an important motif in the Arts and Craft movement fostered by William Morris and hence very fashionable. Oscar Wilde used to decorate his rooms with them and Custance may have been aware of this.

'The gay youth' cannot be her son, Raymond, because the poem was first published in 1902, the year he was born. It could easily be about Bosie, proud like the peacock he is watching, sitting in the sun. Morbidly she muses that he is bound to suffer and die.

Little did she know, in 1902, that much suffering yet awaited her. It could also be about her own youth, which she knows will not last ; one of her common themes in this collection.

One modern critic, Patricia Pulham, has interpreted the poem as describing a 'homoerotic Eden' where a young boy replaces the temptress Eve. She writes that in *Peacocks* « death seems the response to expressions of transgressive desire " and that the 'mood' to which Custance refers in *Peacocks* is a typical end-of-the-century artistic 'mood' that explores homoerotic love. For her the poem is a reflection on Bosie in the days before Wilde's trial, or at least before his death. Bosie is the 'vain and debonair' youth whose beauty tempts a 'disastrous day' where Death will strike dumb Wilde's 'laughing mouth of song'. I believe this is a strained interpretation. The danger with our poetess is that critics always want to relate her work back to Wilde, when she herself was on the whole trying to forget about him. Infact the 'laughing mouth of song' could just as easily be her own, or Bosie's.

Presuming it is a meditation on her husband, it initiates a series of several poems dedicated to Bosie, her boy muse.

Hyacinthus (p. 38)

Originating in Sparta, the Greek mythological Hyacinth was a beautiful youth and lover of the god Apollo, but was also admired by Zephyrus, the west wind. Apollo and Hyacinth took turns throwing the discus. Hyacinth ran to catch it to impress Apollo, but, jealous that Hyacinth preferred Apollo, Zephyrus blew Apollo's discus off course, so that it struck and killed Hyacinth. When he died, Apollo did not allow Hades to claim the youth's body; rather, he made a flower, the hyacinth, from his spilled blood. According to Ovid's account, the tears of Apollo stained the newly formed flower's petals with the sign of his grief. Presumably, Olive associates Bosie with Hyachinth.

Hylas (p. 41)

Hylas was a handsome youth who served as Heracles' companion and lover. His abduction by water nymphs was a theme of ancient art, and has been a perennial subject of Western art in the classical tradition. Hylas was kidnapped by beautiful nymphs and fell in love with one of them, and so the Argos set sail without him, with Heracles grieving the loss of his friend. The parallels with Bosie and Olive are clear enough. He left his world of intimate friendship with men to spend his life with her.

Blue Flowers (p. 42)

Bosie's eyes, of course, were blue.

Madrigal (p. 43)

The references to the fair hair and forget-me-not blue eyes and 'the roses of your body' could so easily make one think this was a rather unoriginal poem addressed to another woman, and indeed written by a man. Except for someone who knows the poet in question. It is clearly to Bosie, full of the perfume of youth.

Endymion (p. 44)

In Greek mythology, Endymion was variously a handsome shepherd, hunter, or king who was said to rule and live at Olympia. Pliny the Elder mentions Endymion as the first human to observe the movements of the moon, which (according to Pliny) accounts for Endymion's love. However, the lover of Selene, the moon, is attributed primarily to an Endymion who was either a shepherd or an astronomer, which profession provides justification for him to spend time beneath the moon.

In 1818 John Keats published his famous *Endymion*, a poem of almost 1,000 lines, whose famous first line is "A thing of beauty is a joy for ever". In Keats' poem, Selene (called Cynthia by Keats) is intially rejected by Endymion but then disguises herself as a mortal and Endymion falls in love with her.

The poetess's Endymion here is no doubt Lord Alfred Douglas, and 'the rapturous descriptions of male beauty' refer to in truth to him, as the couple's friend (and famous promoter of abortion and contraception to the working classes) Marie Carmichael Stopes observed (in *Lord Alfred Douglas: His Poetry and His Personality*, 1949, p. 21) The poetess herself of course is identified with the moon/Cynthia/Selene.

Olive was not the only poet to worship Bosie as the fair Endymion. Two of Lord Alfred Douglas's own poems portray a slumbering Endymion, ultimately revealed as the poet himself, passionately caressed by the moon. One of them, first composed in 1897, but revised in 1908, *The Poet and the Moon*, is unashamedly auto-erotic. All the focus is on the beautiful, sleeping naked boy, diaphanously clothed with the moon's rays.

The moon kisses him 'over and over' until the *stars grow feint* and the *dawn blushes*.

Dance Song (p. 45)

Olive wrote a number of similar poems about the Dance. She saw it as a metaphor for life itself.

A Memory (p. 47)

Clearly not about Bosie, my strong feeling is that this is about John Gray, the Decadent poet, by now a priest, whom Olive met when she was about 16 and when he was in his mid twenties. It reproduces similar sentiments to those found in two separate poems which were entitled 'To John Gray' in the original MSS but published as 'Reminiscences' in *Rainbows* (1902) and 'Ideal' in *Opals* (1897). I believe that in her memories she considered him more beautiful than her husband. Her reference in 'The Inn of Dreams' to her 'fairy Princes' *in the plural* is probably also a reference to him as well as to Bosie. Clearly the image of the young man with whom she became infatuated in 1890 was still very dear to her in about 1905, or even later, when she probably wrote this poem. Unless, that is, it was already written with the other two some time between 1895 and 1901, but overlooked for publication. My contention that it belongs to the period of the first few years of her marriage is based on the impression that it seems to be more recollected and further removed from the events than the other two.

The Photograph (p. 49)

My reading of this is that our poetess has found a photo of herself from days past and is wondering where all the years have gone. She could also be thinking about a lover.

St. Sebastian (p. 51)

For the significance of 'Beauty' see the note for the poem *Primrose Hill*, in reference to St Augustine.

I believe that here our poetess, even if she thinks also of Bosie and his courage, is genuinely moved by the martyrdom of this young man, St Sebastian, standing up for his belief in the truth of Christianity and offering his innocent life in its defence.

It perhaps should be noted that that St Sebastian is famously, and for no better reason than his frequent representation as a beautiful and naked youth, the favourite saint of homosexuals. Oscar Wilde apparently saw and admired Guido Reni's painting of St Sebastian (pictured next to the poem, above) when visiting Genoa. Also, after Wilde's release from Reading Gaol in 1897, he adopted the pseudonym 'Sebastian Melmoth' in France. It is possible, though extremely unlikely, that the sonnet was a kind of memorial to Wilde.

The Magic Mirrors (p. 52)

This is surely a very weak poem, unfortunately, displaying the two main weaknesses of Custance criticised in 1902 after the publication of *Rainbows* : her injudicious use of elipsis and her love of vagueness.

Still, one can guess why she put it at the end of the collection. Having bared her soul throughout the collection, the poetess might – in a kind of girlish modesty – wish to claim that in the end she is an enigma that we cannot really ever understand. In that sense it contains a message similar to her poem *Opals*, which is a better piece of work.

Select Bibliography

Olive Custance (Lady Alfred Douglas)

Brocard Sewell,
Olive Custance : Her Life and Work, 1975.

Olive Custance (ed. Brocard Sewell),
The Selected Poems of Olive Custance, 1995.

Olive Custance (Caspar Wintermans, ed.)
I Desire the Moon: the Diary of Lady Alfred Douglas (Olive Custance) 1905-1910, 2004.

Lord Alfred Douglas

Lord Alfred Douglas,
The Autobiography, 1929.

Caspar Wintermans,
Alfred Douglas : A Poet's Life and His Finest Work, 2007.

Note : Caspar Wintermans is currently working on the publication of the correspondence of Lord and Lady Alfred Douglas.

Acknowledgements

First I want to thank my father, Andrew, who taught me two very important lessons for anyone researching the life of a forgotten poet : perseverance and empathy for the under-dog. Both very British traits which he shares with his great hero, William Cobbett. I hope I have inherited them from him. I grew up largely without television, by paternal dictat, and so due to numerous 'peaceful family home evenings,' where we used to sit reading aloud interesting passages from our various books, I acquired a love of literature very young. My father has also been, I now realise, my best friend and supporter in almost all my madcap schemes. It is about time I thanked him in print, although the immense debt of gratitude I owe him is by no means thereby discharged.

My mother, Joan, grew up in the west of Ireland, the daughter of a merchant tailor, and can remember when she was very young that the maid used to tie ringlets in her hair at night, so that she could be a 'princess'. My father used to call her 'the Queen of the Pixies', which reminds me of Olive and her dreams of fairyland. She is certainly the kindest, most hardworking, loving and long-suffering mother a son could wish for. What is more, she has had the patience to listen to me, holding forth for hours on the subject of this little book.

Then I want to thank Joseph Pearce, the literary biographer. His biographies of Oscar Wilde, Gilbert Keith Chesterton, Hilaire Belloc, Roy Campbell and a host of others have won international critical acclaim. Joe is a very dear friend also. It was while travelling with him in Portugal to interview the now sadly deceased daughters of Roy Campbell (in preparation of Pearce's autobiography of that great poet[70]) that I first got a taste for, and inside knowledge of, literary biography.

It was really a wonderful experience listening to Roy Campbell's daughters : two charming, sensitive old ladies

---

[70] Joseph Pearce, *Bloomsbury and Beyond : the Friends and Enemies of Roy Campbell*.

reminiscing about colourful characters such as Evelyn Waugh and, through the tears, remembering the faults and failings of their eccentric and wonderful parents, of whom Lord and Lady Alfred Douglas remind me a great deal. The Campbells were both, like Bosie and Olive, 'literary converts' (to Catholicism) and had begun their personal journeys with a similarly heart-wrenching mixture of love and libertinism.

Joe also showed me how biography ought to be done : celebrate what makes people interesting and great, not what makes them the same as as everyone else. That is why one can and should be forgiving and kind, as well as thorough.

Another man who takes a similarly enlightened approach to biography is Mr Caspar Wintermans[71]. I thank Mr Wintermans for some kind help and advice he gave me about sources, as well as for providing answers to a couple of niggling questions ; I also thank him for his very thorough and patient work. Labouring in this particular vineyard, one cannot but be aware that one is precariously perched on the shoulders of a giant, albeit a kind one. I feel as though I have climbed up his beanstalk and stolen golden eggs from his kitchen.

Lastly, I want to thank two generous priests whose scholarly attentions have helped to bring this little offering to fruition.

One is the late Father Brocard Sewell, O. Carm., whose monograph on Olive Custance has for forty years been the starting point for anyone interested in the life of the poetess. He provided a springboard without which I would not have dared to jump. I never knew him, but I hope I'll meet him in Heaven, where the two people he said he'd like to meet first were Olive Custance and Canon John Gray.

The other good priest is Father Mark Lawler who, in a break from his interesting doctoral research on Chesterton, read the proofs of this book and suggested some useful amendments. Any surviving infelicities of style and errors of fact are, I must confess, my own.

---

[71] See his *Alfred Douglas : a Poet's Life and His Finest Work* (2007).